I0165982

Gilbert Parker

The Chief Factor

Gilbert Parker

The Chief Factor

ISBN/EAN: 9783741193736

Manufactured in Europe, USA, Canada, Australia, Japa

Cover: Foto ©knipser5 / pixelio.de

Manufactured and distributed by brebook publishing software
(www.brebook.com)

Gilbert Parker

The Chief Factor

THE CHIEF FACTOR.

By GILBERT PARKER.

CHAPTER I.—A COURT OF APPEAL.

SHE was an uncommon girl, and one man, at least, thought her beautiful. He dwelt on the varying colour of her warm golden face, and the way her brown hair lifted with every breath. He knew the difference between her walk and that of the other lasses of Braithen—how free and swaying was her step, how lissom her body. He had watched her now and then as she sat at the loom in old Cowrie Castle, and the picture of her deft fingers, the absorbed intelligence of her face, the slow, rhythmical motions of her arms, and the sight and sound of the flying shuttle, was indelible and delightful. Since he was a lad with the sheep upon the hills she had seemed to him the most wonderful thing in the world. When he grew to be six feet, or nearly so, and his shoulders became wide and his body powerful, he still thought so—and he had learned a deal since the shepherding days. His admiration for her, if not generally known, was at least suspected, and by none more strongly than his old schoolmaster, who had for many years called him, Andrew Venlaw, his most promising pupil; as, indeed, the one lad of whom he had unusual occasion to be proud. The venerable Dominie, little inclined to women as he was, acknowledged in his own mind that there were some points of value in Jean Fordie ; but it would not do to let Andrew know this. He had as great ambitions for Andrew as Andrew had for himself. The lad had not fought his way through pages of barbarous Latin, delusive Greek, bargained with sines and co-sines, imbibed history as a desert does water, and spent midnight hours with archæology, for nothing. He was only a builder of houses now, under a master, but he hoped to be a great architect one day. To that end he had Edinburgh in view ; in Edinburgh, hard work, then success ; then, Jean Fordie, if she would come. And, surely, if he proved himself very much a man, that might count for something with her. He thought no one was good enough for her, but he also thought that none would so worship and care for her as he—that is not an uncommon thing in the love of a staunch and wholesome man. And

70:202

such men also think that a woman is to them an inspiration and an amazing help. The Dominie did not. To him woman was a danger, a disturber of the peace, the flaw in a young man's brain, and more particularly in that of Andrew Venlaw. Occasionally he counted it necessary to lecture Andrew on this. It was noticeable that while his English was excellent on most occasions, and generally so when he began his admonitions, it became provincial as his earnestness increased. Sometimes he bethought himself and reverted to Shakespeare's verbal purity, but he always lapsed again. Once, when he had partially lapsed, thus:

"I'll no say ye've yer ee on ony, Andrew, but ye hae an unco love for the road that a certain lassie travels. And I'll agree there's a bonny glow in her cheek and a licht in her ee, but they're for seein', no for hacin'—no for hacin'. Ye ken you maun gang a lang gate in the warld, Andrew Venlaw, and ye're no sure o' yer footin' for mony a day yet. So where wad ye be wi' a woman and bairns draggin' ye doun?"

How deep these cautions went into Andrew's heart may be judged from the fact that, when it was possible, he went straightway where he could get a glimpse of Jean. For he knew her habits and when she was likely to be seen on the road between Braithen and the Castle.

Sometimes he walked with her, and talked in his blunt but not uneloquent fashion, discussing now the salmon, now the French prisoners of war quartered in the town, or, more frequently, the ballads and tales of the border-side, in which he was well versed. On this last theme he had a keen, almost cultured, and delighted listener; for if there was one thing Jean knew, it was the traditions of the Border—from the date of the first siege of Cowrie Castle and the time when Darnley and Mary quarrelled in the shade of its yews, to the days when Cromwell sent his grim Puritans to it, and cut away a shoulder or so of its masonry, or the gay followers of the Pretender foraged beside it as they marched southward. Jean's knowledge had not come by reading only, but through the oldest and most fascinating channel of—but that will come later!

Andrew had never talked of love to her, however much in his large honest way he had looked it. He knew, indeed, that she did not love him, for he never saw her eye flash warmly in his presence until he touched upon something that interested her; and then the colour would go romping back and

forth in her cheek, and she caught his thoughts almost before he had spoken them. She would turn a glowing eye to his, but it was for the story, not for him. He did not despair, for he had wonderful persistence; he knew that her father, John Fordie, liked him, if not encouraged him; he and she were good friends, and, in a vague way, he believed that it pleased a woman to be loved, so long as the love was not intrusive; and there might come a time! Her brother Bruce and he, however, were not close comrades; and that was unfortunate. Their habits were different, and, what was more than all else, Bruce was the close friend of Brian Kingley, the young Irishman who had come to live with his mother's brother, the Laird of Threep. Between these kinsmen—for one was a poor manager and the other a wild, extravagant lad—they contrived to ruin Threep before the elder man died; so that when Brian came back from the funeral he found the bailiffs in possession, and he was almost penniless upon the world. But while the pennies lasted and credit could he had Brian was not dismayed. And because the gentry became shy of him and he had no taste for tradespeople, he flung himself into the company of the poor farmer and the artisan, among whom he had many admirers. The most notable of these was Bruce Fordie, much to the disgust of his father, who had very stern ideas of life, emphasised, perhaps, by the fact that he was chief gamekeeper on the Cowrie estate, and had charge of the Castle, living there alone with Bruce and Jean, and gathering, unlike them, severity from its strong, unpicturesque solidity. Bruce was a carpenter, but he had only imperfectly followed his trade, preferring idle hours with the French prisoners, and even in defying the game laws, which were as the very Scriptures to his father. The blame of this was placed on Brian's shoulders by John Fordie, though, truth to say, Brian had, in his off-hand fashion, urged Bruce to steady himself by day whatever he did by night.

"For look you here, me boy," said Brian, dropping into his country's brogue, as he always did when with men of the humble sort, "you come of a race that's made for work and not for blether and foolin'; and when you've not done a long turn 'twixt dawn and dusk, you're too full o' blood and old Nick; and bang you'll go with your head at a bailie, or bang 'll go your gun at a hare or a pheasant, when the time isn't right; and your own father 'll trundle you off to gaol, or give you a wipe from behind a hedge."

"Look at yourself!" said Bruce to this.

"Don't I know that? But we Irish are different altogether, by race and by breeding, me boy. Whether we work or play we're in mischief, and it makes but little matter; we're gab and shillelahs mostly anyhow; with fickleness in our eyes for man and maid, and a thirsty throat all the way. We're just the actors and the vagabonds of the world—the luxury of time. We do what we do, and leave undone what we leave undone, as naturally as stealin' a deer or killin' a tyrant. But you Scots, when you play gentlemen of leisure, run amock like any Malay; and that's the truth o' Heaven for you, to take or to lave . . . . and Bruce, me gossoon, there's one more sup, and to led you go, and jump to your work in the mornin'!"

But it was of little use. Bruce was bound to fulfil the apprehensive predictions of the Irishman. On the eve of Beltane Fair, in 1810, he was wanted by the authorities for poaching, and for breaking the head of a gamekeeper, who had somewhat maliciously laid a trap for him and assaulted him unnecessarily. The man was very badly hurt, and if he died it would go fatally hard with Bruce. John Fordie, upright man as he was, openly declared that the boy was now no son of his; and he would, himself, have handed him over to the law, if he could have laid hands on him. Strange to say, the sympathy of the people was more with the son than the father, for the lad had had a way with him at a fair or a wedding, and as pleasant a voice for *Flowers o' the Forest* or *The Bush aboon Traquair* as any south of Edinb'ro town. Besides, there was not in those days as great strictness and religious austerity in the Valley of the Shiel as a hundred years before.

Jean herself, sorrowful and fearful as she was at the news, was not so bowed down in appearance as might have been expected; for, while just eighteen years old, she had a wise head, and she knew well that people like you best and respect you most when you are brave, and not limp of manner nor timid of face. Besides, it was her nature to endure and be courageous; and hard enough she fought her father upon his attitude towards her brother, though respectful in manner and tone always. She had no fear when affection and justice spoke. She urged that he might talk of duty and law as he would, but he had a duty to his son—the duty of protection, which should not be denied, even if the lad did kill a beggarly hare

and wound a fighting gamekeeper. The law, she said, was not justice, and little pause she'd make between the two in a case like this; for law was made by selfish man, and justice by the will of God. That is, as she tried further to explain, the lad would be punished, if caught, infinitely beyond his deserts.

"The will o' God!" retorted her father when she spoke thus, on the eve of Beltane Fair; "the will o' God teaches that ye shall keep the law o' the land. And blude and bane as he is o' me, I'd gie him ower to the bailiff the morn, if he cam within thae wa's; for he has brocht disgrace on me and you, though ye'll no see't. Ye are tae him as if he was a saint oot o' a book, and no' a common wastrel and law-breaker—and murderer too, forbye."

The girl shrank away from these last words as though they buffeted her in the face, but she had iron in her blood. She gathered herself together, determined, as a woman will, to shield the wrong-doer when the tide runs counter.

"You dinna understand," she said. "Can you no' see, faither, that it's flesh and blude tae staun by yer ain flesh and blude whan it's wicked and hunted, mair than whan it's gude and in safety? If Bruce is catched noo he'll be ruined for life. If he escapes there'll be little against him—unless the man dees—for there's nae shame in escaping the law in the warld's een; the shame is in the ither. No' that I'd defend him in the wrong he's dune, and he'll suffer for't mair ways than ane frae noo till the day he dees; but I canna bear to see ane o' my name and his ain faither turn on him, and be willin' to hand him ower to shame and the gallows, maybe." She paused, then she continued, solemnly: "And if I hae tae choose betwixt the sinner and him that'd punish the sinner, I ken what I'll dae, though it break my heart tae dae't."

The girl had been sitting at the loom, in the flickering light of the fire that burned in the huge chimney. For though it was May the air was still slightly chilly, especially in the damp old Castle whose walls were eight feet in thickness; and, besides, the kettle had been hung for John Fordie's supper. The room had but one window, which, of very late years, had been hewn out of the wall. In the suppressed excitement of her last speech, Jean walked over to it and looked down into the shadows of the old courtyard, which were deeper at the gate and where the ruined chapel was fallen to decay above the singing river. The great gateway was open and the gates were gone. Under the hanging ivy and heavy verdure, gathered on the walls and around the old relics of the bartisan tower, might still be seen the crest of the ancient family that had owned it long before the ancestors of the present Earl of Hartfell came into possession; and to right and left of this were small fractures made by the cannon-balls of the Roundheads. Somehow, at this moment, the place seemed desolate to Jean; very hard, stern, and homeless. Indeed, the old castle looked grim enough at night. It stood upright, austere, and strong; surrounded, as it was, by ruins, and flanked by solemn forests. It rose invincible, hoary, and almost sardonic in its unornamented stedfastness, with its one shoulder gone, like some old pensioner of grisly war, alone among dead comrades and an alien world. The soft winds from Margaret's Brae came coquetting with it in summer, the birds made continuous overtures to friendship, the Shiel hummed its variable song to its stones, and the fierce winds of winter ran bouncing down upon it: but it was silent, grey, persistent, and cynical with time. If ever its mouldy coldness was warmed, till some reflection of its old-time memories wakened, it was when Jean's voice had rung in the vaulted chambers—hers and Bruce's, and that of her mother before her. Then, maybe, a king of Scotland walked again in the lofty guest-chamber, and out on the terraces beautiful highborn lasses wandered—gentle, pensive guests, who had here seen bright hours shuttle in and out of life.

The terraces were pleasanter to think of than the dungeons. Often Jean had gone below to look at them, not from any morbid feeling, but because she knew the history of many brave, and sometimes scandalous, men who had lain in these windowless, noisome places. She had lifted up the trap-door of the great draw-well, wondering if it had ever a tragedy also—had been the grave of some adventurous and unlucky visitor. This idea had also possessed Bruce in his younger days, and he—for the well was narrow—had put a candle in his hat, and, with a slight rope attached to his body, had climbed down, as far as he could go, and probed the water with a long stick, while Jean waited overhead. And once, too, when a boy, his father had put him in a dungeon for punishment, and he had (to frighten them when they should come to look for him) actually climbed cautiously down the sides of the well without rope or support of any kind;

and when his father, after searching fruitlessly in great fear, had ascended from the dungeons, he climbed up again and made a great noise. Then they came rushing down, but he was found sitting in the dungeon singing; and he never told them where he had been. After a time they concluded that he had discovered the great subterranean passage which was said to exist; and though he had not done so he was grateful for the idea, and did not rest until he had discovered it; and, fortunately, he kept it secret, for, after many years, it was to be of service to him. He was a madcap lad, quick with his hands and wits too, and Jean to-night, as she stood looking down into the dusk, remembered the many happy days they had had among the hills; and though he was in great danger and she was very sad, some wild prank of his flashing across her mind caused her to laugh outright. Her teeth showed white and brilliant at her red lips, and her eyes were full of a fine-spun fire, so that they glowed finely.

"Aye, aye, ye can lauch," grimly said her father behind her, "but there'll be na lauchin' for him ahint prison doors; and I gie ye my word as a man, if he comes here, I'll hand him ower. Little he thocht o' me, gamekeeper for the Earl, and livin' in his castle, when he went scouring Cowrie lands wi' his gun; for it might hae been me lyin' down in the town wi' a broken head instead o' the ither. . . . But he'll no come here. For I'm telt he's either got awa' across the hill, or is hidin' whaur that wastrel Brian Kingley kens best: twa vagabonds that 'd shame ony place that wasna passed ower to the shame o' Babylon."

And the old man fiercely puffed his pipe, and brought his hand down on the table beside him angrily. Jean wheeled at the window, and very slowly and indignantly said:

"You speak words harsh and wicked too, faither. Brian Kingley and Bruce Fordie are no saints, as we a' ken, but no yin has ever said that they ever did wilfu' malice tae man or woman, or shamed ony but theirsels. Doesn't everyane ken, dinna ye ken, that the keeper brocht on the fightin' wi' Bruce whan there was nae need? An' whatna else is there against him or Brian Kingley, that isna foolish mair than wicked?"

"Oh, I ken weel enough," the old man replied, lapsing, like the Dominie, still further into the provincialism of his shire; though, in general, his education was above men of his class. He had been well schooled, and in the first days of his married life had lived in Edinburgh, where he had married his wife, bringing her with Bruce and Jean to Braithen again. "I ken weel eneuch," he repeated; "the Irish hae smooth tongues, and this yin has juist talkit his fool-talk i' yer lug, so that ye fa' doon and war-ship him. But a wastrel he is and a wastrel he'll be; and ye'll ken o' that some day. Aye, but ye needna look up so shairp at me! Yo hae the stiff-neckedness and temper o' ane that went afore you."

"Ye're speakin' o' my mither!" answered the girl, still keeping her place at the window, her voice determined and more than a little indignant. "Then, if that's sae, though she was yer wife, you maun speak nae more o' her tae me in that fashion. What my mither was to me is mair than she could hae been tae you, faither! I ken ye wadna say ill o' her, but, when ye're angry, as noo, you hae a way o' sneerin'. There's no ane in the glen o' the Shiel but speaks o' her as a gude wife an' a fond mither, and if she didna bend to' yer will, faither, maybe it wasna as ye wad hae't, but it wasna a sin, and it's nae sin in me. For I'll think and act for mysel' when I believe I'm richt."

John Fordie at heart liked this better than unconditional submission, but he was not going to acknowledge it immediately. He blew a great cloud of smoke and replied gruffly, but only with a half-pretended sin-cerity: "Aye, that's the way! There's nae scriptures in the minds o' the young in thae degenerate days. They dinna ken nor care that the Bible says, 'Children, obey your parents;' an' auld age is a thing to be heckled, and lads and lasses at eighteen ken mair than their fathers at saxty."

"No, there ye're only half recht, faither," the girl calmly replied; "for, if the Bible says, 'Children, obey your parents,' it says as weel, 'Parents, provoke not your children to wrath.' Can auld age claim mair respect for itsel' than is due just to auld age? Years dinna aye make folks wise, else old Dave Howden wad ken mair than you, for he is ninety, but he's like a feckless laddie."

"Oh, aye," the other retorted, with a grim chuckle. "However, ye've yer mither's gift o' the gab, and a bit reasonin' too, nane mair . . . And come here, ma lass,' he added with a rude kindness, "for ye're brave eneuch to flee in the face o' Black Fordie, as they ca' him, and I'll no say but accordin' to your lichts ye're richt eneuch, but that's no accordin' to my lichts. There's nae lass sae clever this side o' Forth, and if you wadna

fash yersel' aboot yer raff o' a brither and that Irishman, I'd think there'd be nane yer ckal in a' Scotland:" and again he brought his fist down with a bang.

Jean slowly retreated from the window, came over, and stood in front of her father. But she did no more.

"Weel, hae you nocht to say?" he asked.

Besides the strange fact that she never had a spontaneous affection for her father,—for which there may be shown good and suffi-cient reasons,—she knew that he had not yet softened towards Bruce. She stood motionless, a little apart, and replied: "I've naethin' mair to say than this, that there's trouble upon us, and ye'd mak' that trouble waur wi' yer hardness, faither. Weel, I'm his sister, an' I canna show a' the love I wad to you, gin ye'd do him scaith."

Her eyes swam with tears, but her lips were firm. The old man suddenly rose, his eyes flashing darkly, and his head shaking back his shaggy black hair. He stretched out his arm, and, grasping her shoulder, was about to speak in a loud and angry voice, but she looked him fearlessly in the eye with such affection, sorrow, and indignation mingled, that his anger broke down, and he laughed loudly. "Here's a lass that dares Black Fordie tae his face, and cares nae mair for the grip o' his haun than the Shiel for the clip o' a salmon's tail. Had it been a lunner years ago ye wad hae stude at the market cross, afore a' the folk, for flytin' at yer ain faither; and you wad hae been ta'en ower the coals at the kirk, and I'll no say but ye wad hae deserved it a'." Here he laughed again and looked hard at her. "She's no feard of Black Fordie, she's no feard of the kirk, and she's no feard o' the Bible. . . . And that comes o' the buiks she's read, and the com-pany she's keepit, and o' foreigners wha teach her the folly o' mad kintras, forbye."

"You mean Benoni, of course, faither," the girl said gravely, yet with a new look in her eyes.

"Aye, auld Benoni. Ye listen tae him and his tales. A vaugront, wi' rings in his ears, and a tousseled heed, an' a raree show; that if it wasna for his flute, and the jokes he cracks, wouldna be worth his bite and sup in ony cottage i' the land, far less Cowrie Castle. . . A puir feckless body," he added, peering at the girl as if to read exactly what she thought.

"I ken ye dinna mean thae things ye say about Benoni," she replied smiling. "And ye'll no say them to his face, for, whan he comes, ye sit and listen tae him and his flute

as glaid as me and glaidder. . . . An' why
shouldna I listen tae him and like him?
Ever since I was a wee lassie I've kent him
in and oot o' this place, as I wad
ken ane o' my ain, showman
or no showman."

As if the old man
had quite forgotten

"Brought his hand down on the table beside him angrily."

what he had previously said, he added, less
gruffly and a little abstractedly : " Ye'll
maybe see him the nicht, for the morn is
Beltane."

Fordie suddenly calmed and sat ; the girl
nodded in reply, and went over to the loom
and began weaving.

For a long time nothing was heard save
the flight of the shuttle and the creak of the
pedals ; and the figures of father and
daughter had large shadowy outlines in the
imperfect light. The room looked impreg-
nably solitary. The very solidity of the
masonry, the absence of breaks of any kind
in the wall, and the vaulted floors, gave it a
lonely and prison-like aspect, in which the
loom looked almost like an instrument of

torture, and the girl before it its beautiful
victim.

The building, as we have said, had made
its impress on the man. He had grown
granite-like and sombre; the girl it had made
more imaginative, independent, and grave,
than her years, though her nature was
sanely cheerful.

Now and again as she worked she turned
to look at her father smoking in heavy
silence, or listened towards the window as if
—an impossible thing with those walls—to
catch a step from the courtyard.

The time was moving on to midnight.
They were evidently waiting for someone.
The girl was weary, and the man was dozing
towards the fire, when there suddenly came

a faint roll of rat-tat-tats on the outer door of the Castle, echoing and multiplying as they palpitated up the vaulted staircase.

The girl sprang to her feet; the man grasped the back of a chair beside him, and listened before he rose. She picked up a candle and ran towards the door of the room. "Hark ye, Jean Fordie," said the father darkly, "if it be him that's brocht shame upon us, tell him if he comes within thae wa's or in my sicht, I'll gie him up."

"If it be my brither," she replied firmly yet respectfully, "ye'll no gie him up. And ther'll be hidin' for him forbye, and a bit frae the bread, and frae what mair may be."

"If it be your brither!" he cried angrily. "*If it be your brither,*" he repeated in a strange tone, "why, I'll put a word in your ear." He paused, as if he had been about to say something which had been checked in time. "Well, but gae your ain way, and remember, whate'er comes, that I gae you warning."

"Do not rail, and say what you'll repent. It's mair like to be Benoni than my brither."

Again the sounds blundered up the stairs, and the girl ran through into the darkness, and down to the outer door. She did not ask who was there, but shot back the clanging bolts, dropt the chain, and swung the massive panel open. She was about to lift the candle above her head to see who it was, but a figure swiftly entered, and taking the oak from her hand pushed it to with a jovial force, the sounds boisterously repeating themselves above and below; and then a brusque but most pleasant voice said:

"Well, Jeanie, the old man comes, you see, against Beltane on the morrow. But 'tis a grim welcome you give with a dazed face and never a word from your lips, my dear."

"It's you, Benoni," she responded, "it's you!"

"Yes: whom did you expect?" His

"Good-day to you, sir—Adventurer."

accent was little like either a foreigner or a showman. It was not the voice of a gentleman, yet it had the ring of self-possession, knowledge, and a certain natural fineness, through which merest traces of a humble origin showed. . . . He dropt his hand ever so gently on her shoulder, and his

voice took a softer key, yet not too serious, as he continued: "Perhaps you expected the lad that's been playing too hard and too long these days, and is giving the law a chase?"

"Hoo did you ken, Benoni?" she asked.

"How did I know? You must go to travellers for news, Jeanie. I know that and a deal more, lass."

"Oh, tell me, hae ye seen him ?" she cried eagerly.

"I know where he is," was the reply, "and he's safe enough for the moment, and out of the country he'll be soon, I hope. For the lad's but a mad callant, with no real harm in him, and he that got his head broke brought it on himself."

By this time they were ascending the staircase. "Oh," the girl said anxiously, "I wish you could make my father think that."

The man wheeled upon her gently, a singular look in his face. "He—does—think it," was the slow reply.

"Na, na," she urged, "he's bitter an' hard an' wad gie him up."

"John Fordie would give him up," rejoined the old man, "but he shall not, and he shall change his tune this night, maybe." They were now at the top of the staircase. The old man tapped her hand gently with his fingers, delicate as a woman's, as delicate as hers almost, and not unlike them in shape,—which the girl herself had once noted—and said : "Your heart's in the right place, lassie. It's right, always right. And don't be afraid, for there's many a way out of the woods, if the axe be free in the hand, and the heart and will are strong."

She looked great thankfulness at him. "I ken you will and can dae something for Bruce," she whispered. "Ye're wonderfu', wonderfu' !"

Then they entered the room. Fordie stood where Jean had left him, his pipe still poised, his brow glowering, his face set and hard. When he saw who it was he said bluffly : "It's you, is it, Benoni ? It's you that comes like a ghaist i' the nicht—"

"With a raree show on my back and an empty stomach, and ready to bandy a word with you, Black Fordie ; for it's six months since I crossed the doorstone of Cowrie, or clapped a hand in greeting, and there's my fist as fair to you and yours as it's been these many years."

The gamekeeper towered over the little man heavily, but the latter straightened himself, never a bit daunted by his timid height. Then Fordie said : "I kenned ye'd come ; for whaur the carcases o' Beltane are the Italian eagle hae his hour. But 'tis a bad hour for the lass and me, as you may ken."

Benoni's eyes followed Jean about the room, as she prepared him some supper. After a slight pause he replied : "I do not know that times are so bad that you need

glower like that, Black Fordie. For it's Bruce you're thinking on, I suppose. Be not so fierce nor downcast, for the lad has friends, and the world is wide,—mighty wide I can tell you, I that's travelled it round and round, now here, now there, with a bullet in my leg at Aboukir, a sabre across the arms at Saratoga in the land where the red niggers are, a dig in the ribs in the South Seas from the *kris* of a Malay, and a nasty bruise in Egypt. I tell you, Black Fordie, you're dour over the lad's mishap ; for it's more mishap than mischief. The world has millions not so good as he, as he'll prove to a trick some day."

The little man stretched his legs before the fire, and shook his head in emphasis, so that the gold rings in his ears clinked, and his brown hair tossed on his bronzed forehead. Fordie sat down by the table, and looked hard at the other, but answered never a word : which seeing, Benoni continued : "Mighty wide, as I said, is the world ; and there's chances for him, if he gets clear of the harriers—thousands of chances beyond, better than half-starving here or getting a nasty wind broadside, as he swings towards the trough of misfortune. . . . Didn't I see at Halzie, a few days gone, one from London town, carrying with him a pleasant invitation to a handful of brave adventurous Scot lads, from a great company that owns land in British America, given them by Charles Stuart ? And that man's to be here in Braithen, by my invitation. And what he offers is what I'd take myself, with a merry heart, if I was forty years younger. For, off there, if it's fighting you want, you can get thousands of Indians glad of the chance, and there's millions of beasts and birds free to your gun and your pot, and fish without number. Then, if it's company, there are the gay lads by river and forest,— *les bons royageurs*, they call them, with their pipes and their song ; and Papists though they be, as fine a lot of comrades as ever ran water or land ;—well, there's the country for the wild lads and the idle lads that their fathers deny and the lasses love."

The old man paused and began to hum the chorus of one of the oldest and best-loved songs of the *royageurs*, picked up by him when in Quebec years before :—

> "Sur la feuille ron-don-don-don,
> Sur la joli' joli' feuille ronde."

He had talked much, but not out of sheer garrulousness. He did not wish to give Fordie immediate chances for reply, and he also wished to convey to Jean's mind some fresh comfort and assurance that her brother had a friend on the watch to serve him. She had caught at his purpose, and as she made his supper ready she threw a glance or two of exceeding gratitude to him. With him there she seemed a different being; the painful but beautiful energy of her will seemed relaxed; she was a young girl again; and an amber light, pensively cheerful, floated from her eyes. Benoni, quite unacknowledged to herself, took a place almost higher in her affections than her father—Benoni, the common showman, the flute-player, the vagrom man.

Fordie had remained passive but yet stern. At last he said: "Ye put a fair face on a bad deed, man. I'll nae talk o' the matter the noo, for my mind is made up, and it'll hae no change, whate'er you ken or say. A man that poaches, and bludgeons a gamekeeper's heid is nae son o' mine. I've passed my word, and I'll no leave it."

"And you'll no leave it," remarked the other musingly. Then he flashed an inscrutable look at the other and continued : "You'll leave it some day, Black Fordie, as I've seen many another do, that had as hateful a pride and strong a will. But we'll not quarrel about it now, for there's supper that the best lass in the world has made the sweetest in the land." And he rose.

"Ay," responded the other less grimly, "draw near. The liquor stands waiting, and I'm ready to crack a gossip wi' ye."

Presently, by Benoni's tact, the two men grew warm over talk and tale of the countryside, and of places that Benoni had visited during the past six months ; and then again merged into memories of distant years, participated in by Fordie a little sombrely, by Benoni very cheerfully. From which it may be gathered that Benoni was not an Italian at all. He was indeed of English birth, but had spent his early years in Scotland. What these early years were knew no one in the Shiel Valley except John Fordie knew ; and they were never spoken of anywhere save in Cowrie Castle. There was, as may be guessed, a secret between these two men ; but what it was may, perhaps, be told in its bareness later. It was sufficient, however, to make the men friends ; and though Fordie spoke disrespectfully and petulantly of Benoni to Jean occasionally, the girl knew he did not mean it. But it had appeared to an acute observer that Fordie fretted a little under some clause in the pact of their friendship.

No one south of the Forth knew absolutely that Benoni was not what he represented himself. He had been successfully merged into Benoni the Italian showman and flute-player. He could speak Italian, and it was not strange that, after a great many years in Britain, he should speak English. But these are a few facts of his history :—After a certain trouble had come suddenly upon him, he had gone to London and had sunk into great poverty. There he met one Benoni, a rareo showman, and was befriended by him. Afterwards he befriended the other, and nursed him in his death-sickness. When Benoni died, for immediate means of livelihood he possessed himself of the Italian's show, and to make it more convincing dressed himself in the dead man's clothes, put rings in his ears, and because they were of the same height and somewhat alike in feature, he was able to carry on the harmless imposture. It grew to be a reality ; Benoni was, as it were, re-incarnated ; it was Solmes the Englishman that was dead, Benoni the Italian lived.

He had an abundant humour, a warm heart and a bronzed skin ; he was generous to the poor and to the young ; his show was the best that ever came north over the Border, and he played the flute with an astonishing skill. Next to his presence at Beltane Fair, his flute was most desired and admired ; especially when his services were asked by people (who dreaded not the wrath of the minister) for a dance on the green, or in the Rob Roy inn,—the latter, a most notable function in the history of Braithen.

If there was one thing Black Fordie admired more than another it was Benoni's flute ; for, well as the piper of Braithen played, he was as nothing beside this pseudo-Italian who had sucked up the airs of many lands, and loved to turn them out with his own variations, threading them with the hearty honest vein of a Briton's heart. Benoni's words sometimes struck Fordie with a raw plainness ; he was even afraid of the tongue that had got its game of expression from being tempered on many anvils ; but his flute never gave out any but the most delightful music. It could be as strong as the bagpipes and not as strident, and as soft as the harp with a hundred times its softness.

Sometimes Benoni must be urged to play, for he was subject to impulses ; but to-night he needed no solicitation.

As the men talked Jean had listened long, but at last got up, and went over again to the window, and looked down into the courtyard; for, try as she would, she kept thinking about Bruce and his danger; and she would not have been surprised to see him or feel him looking up at her from the stones below. She looked down. She could see nothing; yet she felt something, she knew not what, it was so vague. It was Andrew Venlaw. She had looked down into his eyes, not seeing them.

Venlaw, knowing of Bruce's peril, and, for her sake, troubling himself about it, had in a purposeless kind of way come out to the Castle, as though in some undefined fashion he might be able to help her or her brother; and, perhaps, get a glimpse of her. He had been over in the hills or he would have come before. He could not call to-night, it was so late; but to be near where she lived was a comfort to him. His lover-like sincerity, though some might call it foolishness, was rewarded. As he stood in the open entrance-gate, one hand resting on the ancient masonry and his face upturned to the lighted window, Jean appeared before it and looked straight down into the dusk where he stood. It was strange to feel the light of her eyes piercing the dark, piercing him, making his heart tremble for joy. Her figure was darkly outlined against the imperfect light behind her; it seemed to have an atmosphere of its own, such as so beautifully surrounds a planet. Only, with her, the atmosphere was lighter than herself—a kind of golden haze which seemed to pass from her person and softly fade into the dim air around her.

She stood there for a few minutes, and he never stirred save to take off his cap with a grave gallantry, as if he were in her absolute presence.

At last he said to her, though scarcely above a whisper, which of course she could not hear,—"For such as you, as the writer says, the world were well lost, for it'd bring something better. And as for death, it wouldn't be so hard to suffer for one that's like the flowers I gathered for you when you were a lassie. Even the wicked can die well where they love well, I'm thinking."

It was at this moment that Benoni lifted his flute and, putting it together, drew from it a sound as true and soft as the note of a divine singer, a full persuasive tone that crept into one's soul, and went swimming gently, royally, through it. At this Jean turned quickly and sat down by the fireplace, and so left Andrew in the dark. But he, catching the music faintly, crept over to the hard walls, until he stood beneath the window, through which it came, though dis-

tantly. The air was familiar and yet all was unfamiliar and uncommon.

Fordie sat blowing clouds of smoke about his sombre face, but not stirring hand or foot; a statue brooding and passive if not complacent. Jean's face was rapt. Benoni played as if he were Amphion causing the stones of Thebes to rear and cement themselves together upon massive walls; as though, indeed, he could bid these walls of Cowrie, in their immense thickness, to crumble and scatter upon the earth.

The candle burned to its socket and he played on.

The fire at last sank to glowing ashes, and the faces of the three were in gloom; but still they sat there, and still the music throbbed about them. It was dark everywhere; but the melody pierced the night, and it had seemed that in that Castle and in all Scotland there was nothing but joy. Yet, not very far away, two men sat together in a hut which they had crept to in the dark, and one said to the other: "Bruce, me boy, out of this you'll have to cut somewhere to-morrow. The break must be made. For I'm certain when you and I and Benoni were talking to-day beyond, some one heard us. The flyin' footstep was there as sure as guns, and, bedad! I thought I caught, too, the flicker of a woman's petticoat, bad 'cess to it! Anyhow they're after you hot-foot, and hiding-places are few. You must make a run for the coast, me boy."

The other laughed a little sardonically and replied: "Brian, lad, I tell you I'll hide at the Castle; for as I said before I ken a way there, kenned by nane else: the old subterranean passage; and once inside the place I'll be safe enough for a day or so, or longer if need be."

"Why not make a bold break straight for the Castle, now, and never mind the passage?"

"You forget that father wouldn't let me in, and besides I warrant the place is watched close enough."

"Right you are, me darlin', the place is watched I doubt not. Well, if it's the passage under ground, luck be with you! And, as I said, I'll join you at Cowrie, goin' myself by the open road. If you once get clear and your foot over the wall of the sea, you'll be right enough again, and Heaven send that, say I."

Bruce's suspicions were right, for, as Andrew Venlaw stood by the wall, he heard a step creeping near, and swinging round he faced an officer, who had suspected him to be Bruce.

In the Castle the old man was still playing; but the notes were faint, and delicately distant.

CHAPTER II.—AT BELTANE FAIR.

As the Dominie, flirting a pinch of snuff at his nose, said—it was a handsome day. From the ancient fort on Margaret's Brae it lilted down upon Braithen; it blew gaily to the Shiel from Glaishen Water; it idled out from the glen of the Weddiners Hope; it spun blithely about High Street in the royal burgh; and it bounded proudly on the fair ground, where the countryside was gathered —hinds and shepherds, craftsmen and farmers, bonnet-lairds, and lasses, from every hamlet in the valley and beyond. A bailie showed his portly form here, and the provost, as became him, loomed, mightily patronising, among the merrymakers. Even a few gentry were present, riding through the mannerly crowd, answering salutes respectful but not obsequious, chatting with each other, and complacently regarding the scene. From all directions clacking carts were arriving, and a heavy coach or two from Edinb'ro way brought visitors. There was plenty of colour, and an amazing heartiness in all. Booths and showmen and pipers were there aplenty, and also all sorts of athletes—wrestlers, putters of the stone, runners, and champions of short-swords, and fantastic gentlemen who played harlequin; but the greatest share of interest was centred at a point where Benoni, in his Italian costume, conducting his raree-show, threw bits of gingerbread among the lads scrambling about him. It was not a stately figure, but it had an air of confidence, of singularity, and character; and was, on the whole, impressive. The velvet of his jacket was old, but it was beautifully clean; his cape, neatly hung upon the framework of the show itself, was well-made, and he boasted a very respectable pair of stockings upon a pair of calves which a younger and a taller man might have been proud to possess. And as for his show, every ring, and bit of metal, and the wood itself, was beautifully polished.

Benoni looked shrewdly but kindly out upon the lads and the crowd at large; a look, indeed, which signified measurement, mastery, and, maybe, a genial sort of contempt: as who does not feel it that has travelled, seen, gathered, and known how like sheep human beings mostly are? Yet there was in him that perfect humour, which is God's salt to nature, lest man should take himself or his little world too seriously. So here and there he dropt a phrase of comment upon men and things about him, now in French, now Spanish, now Polynesian, and very frequently in broad Scotch; the last for his listeners, the others for his own pleasure—for he had a trick of talking to himself. He enjoyed the mystification of those who speculated regarding him, not so many now as formerly. Though he chatted to the idlers about him, and lightly did his professional duties, an acute observer would have noticed that he was watching the outskirts of the crowd and the new arrivals, as if expecting some one. His mind was preoccupied, though he never failed in the point of his immediate remarks.

Presently a fresh horseman appeared on the ground. He had apparently ridden hard. He sat for some time looking at the crowd indolently. His glances rested chiefly on the young men, and not on the young women, as might be expected of one yet to travel the downward incline of years. He presently fixed his eyes upon a stalwart dark-featured young man, standing not far from him. This young man, Andrew Venlaw, was himself scanning the crowd as if searching for somebody. All at once the rider saw Benoni, and said aloud, though to none but himself,—"Ah, my friend of the many languages—the wonderful pantaloon! So he has kept his word, and I've kept mine with him. A marvellous partnership truly, Mr. Ashley Moore; but I owe him something, and he can help me here too." So ruminating he pushed through the people slowly to the showman, raising his hat to those he discommoded. He came within arm's length of Benoni. "Well, signor," he said, "we meet again. Salutations to you!" The voice had a ring of heartiness.

"Good-day to you, sir—Adventurer," said Benoni softly and humorously, casting up his eyes and taking the outstretched hand of the other; "either I've walked hard, or you've dawdled by the way."

"You've mastered our speech fairly, signor; —dawdled is an unusual word in a foreigner's mouth. Still I dawdled, as you say. But I'll not keep you from your fortune-making: this is your golden hive. Your—how should I say it in classic term?"

"Would ariston metron help you?" said the other slyly.

The rider raised his hands in astonishment, not all mockery. "Greek too, signor! Indeed, we're getting on."

"If you've a word for my ear as I have

for yours," said Benoni, lowering his voice; "there's no reason why we should not set the line spinning now, and reel it in at a more convenient hour. I know what you want—a small handful of men of courage and endurance, to complete the list of those going with you to the business of the great Company of Adventurers in the New World."

"You have it pat, signor. 'Tis not every man I want will come, nor every man that'll come I want. This enterprise we are pushing now needs men of girth and substance—body and will;—for the mind, that's not so great a matter. Now, see that strapping youth over there; he looks likely enough; he has a reach of arm, an invincible kind of body, and a massive chin that holds itself well: that's the kind of man for me, and for the Company too, who call for good Scotsmen before all others. For, once out in the wilds, on the neck of the earth as the Hudson Bay country is, whoever go cannot turn back; and either become good soldiers, and trappers, and clerks, and factors, or are our curses, alienating the tribes, trading stealthily for themselves, and flying the brave flag of the H. B. C. on a dirty wind. And there's the truth for you, signor. Now, what about yonder buck?"

"He is what you want and a deal more, sir, but I doubt that you get Andrew Venlaw to go with you. He's a very skilful and learned and ambitious lad, and looks for better—and deserves better—work to his hand than the Arctic regions give."

"Oh, is he then so skilful and learned and ambitious? Then look out, Signor Showman! for such men come into unusual trouble with themselves. I doubt not this same paragon of yours would be glad enough one day, in the sourness and disappointment of his heart, to join our ranks; but then it will be too late. However, I like his looks uncommon well—so well he should be advanced quickly if he'd come—and I'll have my say with him whether or no. For you never can guess what's behind a big serious face like that. There are still women in the world, and where women are masters men are fools." And the rider tossed his horse's mane lightly with his hand.

"One would think you were the old Dominic, speaking so about women; but I'll still be of the opinion that men are the better when women are masters, and know how to rule."

The showman paused. He looked hard at Venlaw, and his mind was full of the scheme the lad cherished regarding Jean—a scheme of which he himself thought well. Presently he continued,—

"Just wait a minute till I clinch the eyes of these lads on my show and take their bawbees. I've one word more for you to think on before we meet again (I hope) this evening. And, while I think of it, I beg you not to go to the Rob Roy inn. It will be overcrowded. But you'll find good fare at the little Salmon's Head there just at the nose of the bridge. I have told them you were like to come. And now this: I can put you on the track of one and maybe two proper fellows, as I hinted days ago; but I caution you they're not quite of those whom the Kirk blesses, nor on whom it thrives. One is a gentleman come to nought through extravagance and wildness, but a man of heart and courage; the other, with too great a taste for adventure in a country of limited freedom, swung his gun shoulderwards at forbidden game, and then cracked the head of a gamekeeper. But he's a lad worth all sorts of trouble, and has sound things in him, I know."

The rider thought a minute, and then responded,—

"You gloze the matter, I see, but what has happened to these men, if they are of the right sort, I promise you shall not influence me against them. For I believe in no man, good or evil, until I have levelled an eye on him, and measured him myself, according to the measure of the H. B. C. And, indeed, I owe you something for a week ago, for I should have been sleeping coldly in that bog at this minute were it not for you. I'll do what I can for these men as freely as you toss your gingerbread among the lads there, if I can."

In a word or two they arranged to meet in the evening at the Salmon's Head, and then the rider, or Mr. Ashley Moore, as he had called himself, nodding pleasantly, moved away through the crowd.

This conversation had been carried on under considerable difficulties, for the showman had all the time attended to his duties, calling out also to the crowd now and then in the interstices of their talk, which was carried on in French, when there appeared to be inquisitive listeners. Now Benoni said, somewhat gravely and sadly to himself as the other left him,—"He wondered about the Greek! The little bits left from that year—that year!" And straightway he went on with his showman's work, but keeping an eye to the rider, and still watching for some one else expected.

The rider came up to Venlaw, and said

pleasantly,—"Good-day to you, Mr. Ven-law."

Andrew looked up slowly, for he had been thinking hard, and responded, scrutinising respectfully the other's face,—"Good-day to you, sir, but I don't remember your face."

"That is probable, but there's no reason why you should not know it and me too in the future ; for I hope we may become better acquainted."

"As to that," said Andrew, drawing himself up a little, "I cannot say, for I do not know what you have in your mind on which to build an acquaintance."

"None other than our mutual benefit; for, listen, Andrew Venlaw, I know the stuff that's in you,—if you will pardon me for saying so—and I know your reputation. Men speak well of you, and, as I judge, rightly so. I have come up here from London looking for staunch, able,—ambitious,—Scotsmen to do men's work in God's country. Well, my friend, Signor Benoni, gave me your name and more besides to your credit. And so, Mr. Venlaw, if you've a mind open to receive good things, I'll pour them into it with a will."

Andrew again looked the other up and down respectfully, and, as if satisfied with his inquisition, glanced over towards Benoni, then back again to his interlocutor, and gravely responded : "I doubt not you are acting for the Hudson's Bay Company of which I have read, and you want men to become their servants and——"

"And their officers and to rule," interposed the other oracularly. "To trade like honest adventurers ; to gain money for themselves and the company ; to fight if need be ; to live a life of activity, courage, and industry ; to *make* a country—the pleasantest, noblest privilege of man."

"You put it bravely, sir," said Andrew, his eyes lighting at the vigour and art of the other's words, " but I fear you and I can do no business; for I must stay in Scotland, which is quite large enough for me—and God's country too, as I think. And I thank you kindly, but we can get nothing by talk with each other, and I beg you, sir, excuse me." And raising his cap, he turned away briskly. The last words were spoken hurriedly. The other's eyes followed him until he joined Jean Foalie, whom he had seen near them just towards the close of the conversation.

At this, Mr. Moore, nodding to himself, said, satirically : "So, there's the spring of his loyalty to Scotland. Well, for such as she

appears I can blame him little ; though I doubt, with a terrible doubt, from the way she meets him, that there's joy on the wing for him there. Better for him if he made success his mistress, instead. For if there's a thing that's like unequal war in the teeth of a man, it is a woman that's got no heart for him, while he's full of love to the eyes for her ; or one that oughtn't to care for him, and does ; or, worse than all, one that's wicked—the millstone round the neck of a mortal. Well, well, we shall see what we shall see ! "

And so saying, he rode away out of the fair ground, up into High Street, and down past the market-cross to the Salmon's Head, where he gave his horse to an ostler, and ordered breakfast ; for, late in the day as it was, he had not yet eaten.

Benoni watched closely the meeting of Andrew and Jean, and commented upon it to himself ; while, at the same time, he amused the people about him by his chaff and playful satire. "No, Andrew," he said beneath his breath, " I fear there's no luck for you there —and that's a wonderful pity, for I'd give my right hand to see it. You're a fine handsome fellow and she'll travel far in the world ere she does better; but you can no more match human beings than you can the birds or the fishes; the human heart is a kittle thing, and women are kittle cattle . . . kittle cattle," and he shook his head very gravely at an astonished lad who was offering him a farthing for gingerbread. "She has an eye —and that's not a business I like—for that mad gentleman, Brian Kingley ; and the end is not easy to see. But he'll be off, I hope, to America soon, and she'll forget him. He cares nothing for her, I'm bound, and that's better for her, dear lass."

Jean's eyes were not for Andrew this morning ; but he did not see that clearly, for women—even the best—do not show their minds with absolute plainness at all times. She had come to the fair, chiefly at Benoni's request ; for he had urged upon her father and herself the wisdom of the action ; so giving colour to a growing supposition that Bruce had escaped to the coast. It was upon the same basis that Benoni had asked Brian to come ; for the opinion was also abroad, that he knew accurately the whereabouts of the hunted youth. The general feeling was, perhaps, in favour of Bruce's escape, especially since it was now believed the gamekeeper would live ; but, nevertheless, there was no diminution in the vigilance and activity of the officers of the law, who were aided in the search by a company of soldiers, garrisoned in the place at the time, and commissioned to assist the civil authority on such interesting occasions.

To Jean, Andrew's emphatic attention this morning was almost irritating, though she was angry with herself because she felt so. While he somewhat stumblingly talked to her, her eyes wandered over the crowd intent yet abstracted. She was the object of much remark, but she seemed to be unconscious of that. She had a proud nature, and much as Bruce's misdoing and danger fretted her, she still could look fearlessly in the eyes of the world ; for, young as she was, she had arrived at the knowledge that its condemnation or momentary execration could not affect a life in the long run. This had been somewhat due to the teaching of Benoni, who, showman as he was, had probed the heart of the big masquerade, which is only reality by the family hearthstone and in the closet. Jean possessed uncommon courage, as the after-events of her life showed ; and she was so little self-conscious that she did not realise how much an object of interest she was, until her father, heavy-browed, and massive as usual, stalked through the crowd towards her. Then she appeared to see the equivocal looks cast upon them both, and heard women—of less beauty than herself— jeer at her ; while one close behind her said to another : "See, Elsie, she's set oot like a peacock's feather, and struttin' i' pride, and her ain brither's a poacher, and a' but a murderer, whiles. She'll no wark i' the mills wi' the ither lasses, weavin' like yoursel', Elsie ; but just has her ain loom i' the Castle as 'twere the harp o' a lady o' blood, forbye, the minx ! "

Venlaw heard these words, and he winced under them, then grew indignant, his face flushing hotly. But Jean, who had also heard, said to him quietly : "She doesna mean it, Andrew ; it's only that she likes sayin' bitter things."

Black Fordie approached them, his face lighting up as he saw Andrew, and he clapped his hand on the young man's shoulder, with the words : "Good-day to you, lad. I'm prood to see that ye dinna turn yer back on an auld frien' like some I ken,"—and he glanced about him—"like some worthies— and fools, I ken," he added ; "and at Cowrie Castle, whaur ye're fain to come, I ken, we'll be aye glad to gie ye bit welcome, though we're less by ane than when you cam last ; and we'll be aye less by that ane, whatever ! "

Venlaw grasped the other's hand and said

a manly word or two ; but what they were he could not tell, for his mind was full of the general significance of the event. This emphatic greeting while he was with Jean in public, the almost ostentatious clasp of possession in the old man's hand on his shoulder, his words of decisive invitation, started in him a throbbing sense of delight. The incident had been watched by many, and knowing, as they did, that Andrew had never shown preference for anyone in the valley but Jean, and that Black Fordie had admitted no one as a suitor heretofore, it was almost like an acknowledgment of Andrew's acceptance as a son-in-law. Jean felt the position too, and shrank almost perceptibly from it ; and her eye wandered over the throng again with a hint of present trouble in it. But she stood very still and talked to Andrew, as impassively as she could. Andrew saw her wandering look, and, with the acuteness of the lover, guessed whom she was seeking. He knew, though he had seen Brian and the girl very little together, that Jean was not unimpressionable where the Irishman was concerned. He had regarded it as the fascination which a man of gentle birth and graces of manner has for a girl, lowly born, but with instincts and capacities above her rank ; and he had always assured himself that it was a mere passing fancy ; for Brian, himself, seemed never to pay her more attention than any other woman. Had Andrew known that this was all the more likely to raise the flame in Jean's heart, he would have been more apprehensive.

But there was one whose concern regarding that incident with Black Fordie was more notable than that of either Andrew or Jean. Elsie Garvan, to whom the scandalised critic had just been calling Jean a minx, had an angry and disturbed heart this morning. In so far as Venlaw liked Jean Fordie, she disliked her ; and a disappointed and bitter woman is not of pleasant or profitable company in the world. Of a strong, hearty, but bold kind of beauty, Elsie had a strain of hardness in her ; and it would give her nerve to do a cruel thing, if tempted greatly. Ever since a child she had cared for Andrew Venlaw ; and now she would give half her lifetime to have him look at her as he was looking at Jean. Many a Sunday she had (at first, hesitatingly, shyly,) placed herself in his way as he came from church ; and again on week-days, as he went to and from his work ; but she never had got from him more than the simple greetings and companionable interchanges of friendly acquain-

"Ay, we are baith fules, Pete."

tances. She was a girl of many resources, and she persisted; for, to her, love was a game, and she played it crudely, but heartily and hungrily. She saw no harm in doing her utmost to win the man she loved; and many another lass of higher degree has thought and acted the same up to this point in her career. It may be that the well-born lady has even gone as far as Elsie soon would go. For this girl had a weapon in her hand, given her yesterday by the irony of chance. Brian had hinted about this weapon to Bruce last night in the conversation we reported, but he did not know who held it;—and that was a pity, for Brian was a man of as many resources as Elsie, and he could use them in more delicate fashion, when need be.

Elsie, as she watched Jean and Venlaw, shook back her loose dark hair with an impatient gesture; her teeth caught in a cruel emphasis, and she suddenly turned away. She threaded the crowd silently, passing out of the fair-ground, and making towards the river-side, where she walked up and down, debating with herself upon a question that troubled her mind. She knew of Bruce's hiding-place. It was her skirts which had been seen on the margin of the old quarry. She had the Scotswoman's sense of compassion for the hunted; the strain of Border kindness was as strong and valiant in her as sanctuary is in the veins of the Corsican: but she loved; and to some, love, on occasion, is madness. She had the hateful faculty for jealousy—that most potent criminal. The struggle went on in her for a long time; and when she returned to the fair-ground she had not made up her mind; for she was not so sure—and this was the lowest and coarsest of her hesitations—that Bruce's capture would weigh with Andrew; and she was not yet so malicious that she could do this hard thing to Jean out of mere hatred.

To the fair-going people the day had been most propitious; and Bruce's affairs and the presence of his sister and father had given a spice of piquancy to the general event. Benoni, ever watchful, worked in Bruce's interest by dropping a hint here and there that the lad had doubled on his hunters and escaped. In course of time Black Fordie disappeared from the ground

2

to go to some part of the Cowrie estate; from which he did not expect to return for a couple of days; but Benoni was to live at the Castle, so that the girl would not be entirely alone. In early afternoon, Brian appeared. He was in high spirits;—for he had been drinking a little—dropping a word of humour to the meanest, and apparently oblivious that he was eyed askance by the staid worthies of the community, regarded coldly by the few gentry who still watched the proceedings good-naturedly, and followed somewhat suspiciously by officers of the law, who could not yet credit the news that Bruce had escaped, while they were certain Brian had knowledge of the youth's whereabouts.

They had gone too far afield. Bruce was at their very doors. The hut over the quarry communicated with a hiding-place used by fugitives hundreds of years before—the underground cell of an old monastery. While not far from this again was the traditional subterranean passage to the Castle, necessary in past days when there was more war than peace; and a not uncommon thing in modern times, for Prince Joseph Bonaparte had one of considerable length at his place of exile at Bordentown, New Jersey.

Presently Brian drew near Benoni, and after a few casual remarks, said almost beneath his breath : " Well, have you seen him ?"

"Yes," was the quick reply, " you're to meet him at the Salmon's Head, at eight o'clock; and he'll arrange with you about Bruce."

"Sure, you've the root of the matter in you, Benoni," responded Brian, admiringly.

"I'd think more of you if you'd fight shyer of the liquor, at a time like this," rejoined the old man.

Brian snapped his fingers lightly, and replied : " Bedad, I don't live by your thinkin', Benoni; but you're a sound old rascal, and we'll not quarrel."

"Can you manage about the horses ?" the other anxiously asked.

"I can that. I've got him relays over the hills, and once he's on the way he can go like the wind to Dunbar—if that's the place from where he ships."

Moore, the officer of the Hudson Bay Company, had returned to the fair-ground, and when he saw Brian in conversation with Benoni, said to himself : "That's the wild Irishman, I suppose. He has the look of a man; and I've known a few skirmishes with Indians and a season of arctic frost take the

devilment out of the wildest. We could tame even him, I think. He's a handsome lad, in spite of the liquor that's in him."

An hour later Beltane was at its apogee. The booths were doing an immense business, dancing was going on, and through the sun and the innocent if boisterous mirth, the Shiel sang its slow but tuneful song, crooning unchangingly through the enjoyment. The very hill-sides above, aglow with gorse and heather, spread with a carpet of gold and purple, seemed alive with enjoyment.

Groups were presently seen moving towards Benoni. Some one had at last persuaded him to bring forth his flute. He stood with his back to the show, a clear space about him,—for he would not play unless,—and eager callants were clearing a still larger circle for a dance to Benoni's flute, always the choicest feature of Beltane Fair. This accomplished, each set about getting his partner. Venlaw stood near Jean. Not with a disposition regarding gaiety different from girls of her age, Jean was, also, the best dancer in the Shiel valley,—a matter to be understood by any that once saw her. She was all natural grace and lightness. To-day, however, if she danced, it would be because she had promised Benoni to do the same as she had done in the past: besides her father wished it also. As to her partner, her father, before leaving, had said she must dance with Andrew. There were only two men she cared to dance with at all; one clasping her would give her joy; the other,—well, it was only Andrew Venlaw, her old friend, and it was different from dancing with any respectable lad simply because he asked her. If Brian only would ask her! She did not let herself think of it; and yet she wanted to question him about Bruce; that seemed a justification for her wishing it. Andrew was little of a dancer, but he wanted to dance with Jean to-day before them all; firstly, to clinch his show of sympathy and friendship with her; and secondly, to feel for a moment that clasp of possession which he would have given worlds to make permanent. But this last thought held him back for a moment. He blushed at it. Yet he was determined, though he hesitated for an instant. His hesitation was, perhaps, the cause of all the after trouble. At the very moment that he turned to ask Jean, Brian Kingley appeared on the outside of the little throng about them. He had had more drink, still he was not wholly intoxicated. Obeying a sudden and overmastering impulse, impossible to account for, save by an underground spirit of jealousy, which, as yet, he had no right to exercise, he pushed in towards the two. He caught Jean's eye just as she gave her hand to Andrew. A young bonnet-laird, standing beside Brian, said to him with pointed humour,—"There's metal for you, man; take her away from the gowk. Look: her eye is on you."

This was the undefined thought in Brian's mind. Without a word he strode forward quickly, caught the hand lightly away from Venlaw, swung Jean gently to him, and carried her off in the trail of the music, which had instantly changed with this action to a swifter measure, on a weird intonation. Any watching Benoni at that moment would have seen that his lips twitched over the instrument and that his eyes gave out a strange red light; but he played on.

The Hudson's Bay officer, standing not far, started, and murmured to himself : "There's more in this than swells to the eye; I'm not sure yet that I've lost you, master Venlaw."

Venlaw stood for a moment dazed; but his hands clinched when he saw Brian's mocking face turned on him as the two whirled by him. He went white, then red, and took a step forward. Jean's face was pale, and a strange glow ran on it. She was very grave, her nostrils quivered slightly, and her eyes shone dark. Suddenly Mr. Moore, who was watching her face remarked to himself the strange likeness here was at this moment between the girl and old Benoni. He pronounced it drcll, but certainly there was something in it.

The dancing of the two lasted for a minute or so only, but while it was on Brian whispered swiftly to Jean concerning her brother, and then, stopping the dance, lightly let her go. But, as if on second thought, and with a mad impulse, he reached out, caught her in his arms, and kissed her full on the lips, and then stept back. Under this action the girl held herself together firmly, yet in a most troubled fashion too. Her face was full of a pained sweetness, though she made no resistance whatever. But when it was over she shuddered slightly.

"And so, faith, Jean Fordie," said Brian aloud, evidently referring to his services for Bruce, "do we levy on our debtors in Ireland, and give them absolution thereby;" and he lifted his hat to her, looked at Venlaw with a malicious playfulness, and was about to turn away, amid the astonished exclamations of the crowd.

But Venlaw stepped forward and caught him by the shoulder. "You coward! you

coward!" he said in low wrath, "is it the fashion in Ireland to insult the sister as well as ruin the brother?"

Brian had swung himself away from the savage restraint of the hand, and stood flushed, but yet cool enough, a foot or two away.

Benoni, his eyes steadily regarding the group fixedly, played on without pause but shrilly and weirdly. The Irishman tossed his head slightly, and retorted : "You're a bit free with your hand, young Venlaw, and a trifle too glib with your tongue. Now, I'll tell you what we don't do in Ireland, we don't answer questions to every raff that asks them, nor reckon to every jealous man, when we've proved him to be of little account. . . . And so good-day to you, Venlaw!"

"No, sir; but it is not good-day," said Andrew, stepping in front of him. "You have insulted the daughter of my friend, and the sister of yours ——"

"For which I'll answer to your friend and my friend, but not to you, my lad," interrupted Brian coolly.

"You'll answer to me first for a coward's trick——"

"In taking Miss Jean Fordie out of your arms! But all's fair in—war such as this, my shepherd lad. Besides, what says the lady herself? Does she ask you to stand to her cause with arms all twitching so?"

Venlaw turned now, amazed and full of doubt, to Jean, who stood looking at them as if she were in a dream; but she said nothing.

"You see, you've proved yourself but a meddling youngster, after all, Venlaw," said the other with a slight sneer,—"a meddler and a fool."

At this Andrew, white to the lips, and maddened by the circumstance and by the remarks of some bystanders, raised his arm to strike, but Jean caught it with a cry of pain. "No, no! for God's sake, no!" she exclaimed.

Venlaw paused as if himself struck, and turned and looked her straight in the eyes. Hers did not drop before his, but she flushed deeply. After an instant she cried : "Would you disgrace me by fighting? Go, both of you, go, and forget it all—all!"

Had Brian not been somewhat in liquor it is hard to tell what impulse for reparation might then have come to him, for he was more wild than wicked. But he knew that Venlaw hated him, he had no love for Venlaw, and he enjoyed the other's discomfiture.

Besides, in his excited condition, he did not count the thing as serious, since he had kissed more than one girl publicly in his time, though never one quite like Jean Fordie, as he acknowledged afterwards with regret.

He raised his hat now and said: "It would look ill to fight before a lady, but if you'll meet me some other day, Venlaw— eh?"

"When? Where?" replied the other viciously.

Brian at that moment caught Mr. Moore's eye, and with a sudden inspiration, and in mocking cadence, said: "Faith, let it be at the North Pole or thereabouts. You'll fight better where it's cool, my firebrand!"

And swinging on his heel he strode away. The music as suddenly stopped, and Benoni thrust his flute into his pocket, and silently fumbled with his show, keeping his eyes steadied, however, on Andrew and Jean. With the stopping of the music there was motion and much talking. The scene suddenly became changed; the feeling of the incident was rendered inclement; to Jean unbearable. She went to Benoni and said: "I am going to the Castle. You are coming to-night?"

He did not speak. He nodded assent kindly, and looked at her earnestly, encouragingly, from under his shaggy brows. She turned away, and an instant after Benoni, still watching her, was, however, laughing and joking with the crowd, doing his best to dispel the scene from their minds. Indeed, on second thought, he took out his flute and began to play, and soon the crowd were dancing again with all their might.

CHAPTER III.—"FOR LOCHABER NO MORE."

ANDREW had started to follow Jean, but he suddenly turned away, elbowed himself through the crowd, moved across the green and up High Street towards Dominie Dryhope's cottage. Someone followed him. Presently, as he wheeled into a side street, that someone came closer to him. It was Elsie Garvan. She had seen, with a harsh delight, the incident on the fair-ground. The game seemed to have been given over into her hands. What now came to her mind shocked her at first, it was so cruel, so untrue; but she had not been brought up under a mother's care, and she was tolerably bitter against life all round. She had an idiot brother, Pete, whom she had to care for and support alone; she had no other relatives. If

love had been given her happily it might have transformed her. It was given her unhappily and she became capable of a wicked thing. Her nature was headstrong; her heart was a place of conflicting, almost aboriginal, passions. All that she saw now was an opportunity to visit punishment on her rival. If it succeeded, as she intended, it meant that Andrew should be estranged from Jean, and might, therefore, turn to her who had loved him ever since he had fished her, nearly drowned, out of the Shiel, when they were children.

She knew that Bruce Fordie would try to go to the Castle this night by the subterranean passage. She knew that Brian also would go there, and that Black Fordie would be absent. The first two of these facts she had learned—(really by accident, for, passing the old quarry, she had caught a glimpse of Brian and Benoni, and followed them more out of curiosity than anything else)—from Brian, Benoni, and Bruce themselves; the last she had heard Jean's father declare on the fair-ground. As may be seen, the opportunity might have been grasped by a mind less acute than Elsie's.

Before Andrew reached the Dominie cottage she hurried on to him, and touched his arm. "Andrew Venlaw," she said, "hae a word for ye."

He turned abruptly to her, his face angry and hard.

"We used to be frien's, Andrew," she continued, "and are yet, I'm thinkin'. An because we were and are, I'd tell ye, as frien', o' a thing that concerns ye." She paused.

"Go on, Elsie," he said, not very heartily.

"Promise me, that whatever I say ye'll no be fierce wi' me."

"No man is fierce wi' a woman," he replied gravely.

"I ken," she continued, "and a' Braithe kens what ye hae thocht o' Jean Ford this lang time. And a man hae a richt to think o' what woman he wills——"

"What's this to you, Elsie?" he quickly interrupted; "or to ony i' Braithen?"

"It's naething to me," she retorted wit sudden anger; "but I'm yer frien', and h been lang syne. And this I'll tell you"— here she set the whole desperate game upo one throw—"that ye saw ae thing the da and I'll show ye anither the nicht, if ye h a mind——"

"What do you mean, Elsie Garvan, by ' saw ae thing the day, and ye'll show me anith the nicht?' In God's name, speak!"

She spoke with slow, cold emphasis, as though her heart had suddenly congealed, and she was now merely the pitiless surgeon to his misfortune. "He kissed her on the lips, and she made nae shame o't, but when ye'd hae him fecht caught yer airm just ye should strike him—you are the heavier man. D'ye think she wad hae caught *his* arm waur ho gau'en to strike you?"

Venlaw's face was not pleasant to see. A hundred little things flashed through his mind—little unsubstantial things; trifles fast becoming confirmation strong as Holy Writ. He spoke no word, but nodded savagely.

She went on. "Well, d'ye think ony girl would let that kind o' thing on tho open fair-ground, frae sic a man,—frae a gentleman, and we ken what kind o' a gentleman—if—if he hadna don' 't afore, whaur it wasna sae open, whiles——"

She paused again. She had the native instinct of tho artist in cruelty, of the surgeon who loved the work for its own sake.

"Go on," he said, huskily.

She continued : "Of course Bruce Fordie was his frien' ; and, of course, that was his way to ken Jean better. And noo that her brither is disgraced, and her faither no there, ho shames her afore them a' ; for that de'il is in him that looks upon a woman's heart as a matter for idle days."

He spoke now with a strange, hard calmness : "Elsie, you hae a bitter and a dreadful tongue—you said '*the nicht ;*' that there was something concerning the nicht!"

"You always were impatient, Andrew," she responded, with a voice tuned to a pretended compassion, "and stubborn, too, else ye'd hae seen what ithers saw, and——"

His face was very pale. "If you don't stop torturing me, and tell me what you mean by '*the nicht,*' there'll be some words that ye'll no care to hear, nor I to speak."

She saw that she had gone as far as she dared. "Well, then," she said, "meet me tho nicht in tho last clump o' yews afore ye come to the Castle yett, and I'll show ye what I mean."

"No, but you shall tell me noo," he sternly urged, as she made now to leave him ; "for I ken there are mair evil things hanging on your tongue. So, say them and ha'e done wi't!"

"'Deed, then, I'll no be bullied into sayin't," she retorted, "until it please me, Andrew Venlaw. But I tell ye, that if you meet me tho nicht, ye shall see the meaning o' what happened tho day. Jean will be alane at the Castle for hours. Durin' that

time someane 'll cam to her. Andrew, lad, I hae sorrow enough for you, but you maunna tak' it tae heart, for there's them in the warl' that's true, for a' there's them that's fause."

"Why do you talk," he responded, with a despairing bitterness, "as if Jean Fordie were breakin' faith wi' me ? She hasna promised to me ; she's free to wha she wills."

"Ay, Andrew, and she wills freely," said the other, with a cynical laugh.

"If you were a man," he replied, grimly, "I'd hae choked that laugh back in yer throat. But ye're a woman, Elsie Garvan, and you were a frien' o' mine, and I dinna doubt ye mean nae harm."

"I mean to be your frien', and I speak to you as ane, Andrew ; it little do we, who think weel o' you, like to see ye throw yer heart awa whaur it isna deserved."

"Maybe that speech would come fitter frae a man," he remarked with irony.

"Ay, if ony man kenned what I ken," was tho smooth reply. "Is it your will to meet me or no ?"

"I'll meet you," he replied, "at tho time you say."

He was about to turn abruptly from her, but paused, held out his hand, and said : "I ken you've meant to be a frien' to me, Elsie, but it's bitter kindness you serve me."

"Better that you should have it frae a frien' than an enemy, Andrew," she replied in a low, insinuating voice, her big hot eyes swimming with his.

He left her, and instead of going to tho Dominie's place wheeled, and went to his own lonely cottage.

She sauntered slowly o'er the brae towards her cottage and her idiot brother, and, as she crossed the threshold, a shudder went through her, for she felt for the first time how different even the meanest, most wretched home appears, when one has done a wicked thing. It rises up—all its associations rise up—as if in piteous shame, to wave us back. When that feeling ceases wholly in the heart, and the home can be entered without remorseful diffidence by the erring, that man or woman is lost. Elsie had had little brightness in the world, yet this idiot boy, lolling on the hearthstone beside the old crone who cared for him when his sister was absent, she had loved in a hungering sort of fashion. She had talked to him as to a faithful animal, getting no sane reply,—only a sympathy, not higher than Caliban's, not lower than that of a hound. She sat down beside him now. He caught at her hand and rubbed his fat burning cheek against it, and said : "O little she—O puir Pete—her eyes a' fire—O, O, puir Else, puir Else—rat in a hole the day—Pete ride a white horse—O, Else—puir Pete's pretty fule—O, O, amen—flee awa' to God!"

She shivered, caught the idiot's head to her knee. "Hush, hush, Pete!" she whispered. Then, after a moment: "Ay, we are baith fules, Pete."

At eight o'clock, as arranged, Brian was sitting in the Salmon's Head waiting for Moore to come. He was in no buoyant mood now. "A beggarly trick it was," he said aloud. "The devil was in me. But when I saw him with his Scotch conceit, as sure of her as if they were hand in glove at the altar, I couldn't resist it. Bedad, though, I wish it had been any other than Bruce's sister. Still, 'twas only a kiss after all; and I'll make it up to him one way or another. But how? By words as easy to the Irish tongue as wind to the hills? Anyhow, I'm doing him a turn with the last of my money, and I'll get him away if I can. Well, well, but I'm a bit of a scamp!—and what's to become of me is a riddle for heaven to solve." He dropped into silence; then, after a moment, he sprang to his feet, and marching up and down the room, said excitedly: "I'll do it, as it flashed into my mind on the fairground; I'll go to the North Pole, or wherever that Hudson's Bay country is, and live with the bears or die fighting the Indians, and there you are, Brian Kingley, gentleman!"

"I don't see the necessity for either," coolly said a voice behind him.

Brian turned and saw Mr. Moore.

"As I said, I don't see the need for either. Come to the Hudson's Bay country, then, by all means; for though you've been a bit rash with your own money, there's no reason why you should be so with other people's; and though you're something hasty with the lasses, age and fighting and the H. B. C. will mend that. And if you'll give your word and come, I'll take the risk with you, though it's no light matter."

"Faith, you're mighty kind, and something forward and lofty, too," responded Brian with dignity, but not without humour. "A man may lift a tumbler, and kiss a lass, and squander a fortune, but he may know without telling, and keep without assurance, the fashion and character of a gentleman." He drummed his fingers lightly on the table before him, and looked the other steadily in the eyes.

"Why, now," replied Moore, "I beg your pardon. Maybe it'd be impertinent for me to say that I like you better for that speech, but I do. And because I'm as well born as yourself, and have squandered money and had my wild days with the lassies,—more wild than bad, I hope—though you see my hair is wintry now at the temples, here is my hand if you'll take it, and, in the name of the H. B. C., I offer you a place also."

They shook hands. Brian motioned the other to a chair, and they sat down. Mr. Moore continued:

"I know you want help for a friend of yours and Benoni, who'd be well out of this tight little island; and though it's a risk I shouldn't care to take every day, still I'm ready for it. For, Benoni did me a good turn, and I fancy favour for favour."

Explanations then ensued, and arrangements were completed, by which Bruce, if possible, should join Mr. Moore at Dunbar, whence a vessel sailed to London, there to board one of two vessels intended to proceed to Hudson's Bay within a few weeks of each other.

As they sat there Benoni entered quietly. He was greeted warmly by both men, but he answered them in subdued fashion. The shrewd humour seemed to have fled suddenly from his tongue. He looked kindly enough at Mr. Moore, however, and at once entered into the question of Bruce's escape and his subsequent destination. At last he turned to Brian and said: "You did a hateful trick to-day, Mr. Kingley,—one that should cause you sorrow to your grave."

"Faith, sorry enough I am at this minute, Benoni, but—" here he reached over to take the old man's arm in good-nature; at which the other drew back—"but 't was only a mad and idle prank."

"'Tis mad and idle pranks that ruin the world. You were born a gentleman, sir; you should have remained one, and done better by the sister of your friend."

Brian kept down his temper, though he thought Benoni was taking the matter far too seriously. "I should have been anything but Brian Kingley to-day," he rejoined with a laugh. "Sure, though, you're something of an old meddler, Benoni. You have too fatherly a care of the ladies. I doubt not but when you were young yourself you cast an arm about a lass like Jean Fordie, and——"

"Like Jean Fordie," and a singular light came into the showman's eyes as he caught his cloak and threw it a little grandly over his shoulders, drawing himself up at the same time,—"as like her as you like your shadow, man; but the twist of my arm was honest, and her honour was my honour."

Here he came close to Brian. "If a man did that to her that you did to Jean Fordie to-day, and I'd cared for her as Venlaw does for the lass, the deed would be paid for in good round coin, young gentleman."

Brian was a little irritated now. He thought too much was being made of the occurrence. "Well, then, this shall be paid for in good round coin, Signor Benoni, chief of go-betweens!"

"More than you think for—much more. You are not dead yet. I've lived long and travelled far——"

"From the figs and pipes of Palermo to the flags and flutes of Braithen," interposed the other nonchalantly, and with an attempt at wit.

"—And travelled far, as I said, and I never saw a man who did an idle or ill turn to a woman who didn't face it again, a thousand times, to his confusion."

"Faith, it's very fine English you use, for a poor Italian, the keeper of a raree show." And now the Irishman said what he did not mean, because, in his dare-devil spirit, he saw a fighting light in Benoni's eye. "But women? I'm thinking you set them a ladder too high; and for such a young hill-bird as Jean Fordie, with a lilt to her eye and a toss to her skirts——"

He got no further, for the showman sprang forward and caught him by the throat with his strenuous, delicate hands, and shook him savagely. Then suddenly letting him go, he fell back to the wall glowering, in an attitude of defence, fury still in his fingers.

Brian was so taken aback that he had scarcely raised his arms in attempt to snatch the assaulting hands away, and now he stood looking with more surprise than anger at Benoni. He put his hand to his throat, and then stretched up his neck.

"Indeed," said he, "you're the first that ever had his hands there, my man; and an hour ago, I'd have said he that did it should toss in a nasty cradle." Then, with a sudden rush of rage,—"and by Heaven——"

Here Mr. Moore interposed: "No, no, Mr. Kingley, the man's old, and you were foolish in what you said. You spoke slightingly of women, and he's done no more than many would have done; though I'll admit, and I hope he will, that he provoked you uncommonly."

"But what, in the name of St. Patrick, are all women to him? and wherein does Jean Fordie concern him so closely?" cried Brian, still chafing.

The old man came forward. "I had no

right to catch you by the throat, Brian Kingley," he said. "I only remembered that I had eaten at Black Fordie's table, and been cared for by his daughter when I had a sickness and——"

"And here's my hand, Benoni, if you'll take it. For I was all wrong and you were all right. And I swear to you that I meant no harm in what I said nor in what I did to-day. For Bruce Fordie is my friend, as you know so well, and I'm a rapscallion that needs——"

"That needs to tread the neck of the world, to rule the north, for the brave company of Adventurers trading in Hudson's Bay," said Mr. Moore, completing the sentence.

Then with a manly apology Brian shook hands with Benoni, and they proceeded with their conference concerning Bruce.

Braithen was making merry by night as it had been gay by day. At the Rob Roy inn jocund feet were responding to the scrape of an indifferent fiddle in one room, to the pipes in another, and to Benoni's flute in a third. In Cowrie Castle one window was alight. We have seen both the light and the window before. Within the sombre but comfortable room Jean sits in the corner weaving. She had tried to read, but she could not fix her mind upon the words. She went to the window and looked out many times until it grew altogether dusk, then she dropped the blind and lit the candles. The fact that she dropped the blind was unusual. But Brian had whispered in her ear that day the possibility of Bruce coming, and there must be no exposed windows. Brian had said also that he was coming to see Bruce, but at this moment she had no pleasure in that. It gave her, rather, infinite pain. She could hear even more plainly with her weaving than without, as those may know who have lived by the monotonous wash of a sea, or near the low rumble of machinery. Extraneous sounds pierced the rhythmical vibrations of the loom with a singular distinctness. At last, to the swaying of the weft before her, she sang an old song softly to herself, the sounds echoing softly and plaintively through the room :—

" It wasna that ye loe'd me, O my dearie,—
   Your een lookit never sae tae me ;
 But I loe ye an' my heart's aye weary,
   Syne the hour that ye gang frae me—
     O my dearie, come back tae me ! "

She sang two or three verses, then she threw her head forward on her arms. "Oh! oh!" she murmured, "why did he do't? Why did he do't ? There'll be trouble come frac't——How I wish I could hate him——!" Presently she started up, as though she heard a sound. She ran to the door, opened it and listened. There was nothing. She went back and sat down. It was eleven o'clock. Not long after she heard a pebble rattle on the window, then a knocking, not loud. She took up the candle and hurried down-stairs. She asked who was there. Brian answered. For an instant she hesitated, then opened the door. Brian stepped inside.

"Is he here yet ?" he asked.

"You mean Bruce?" she said breathlessly.

"Yes. I tried to make you understand when we were dancing. You know of the old subterranean passage from the quarry to the Castle ?"

"Yes, yes : Bruce and I explored a part of it when we were children."

"Well, we knew it wasn't safe for Bruce to stay any longer where he was. So he determined to try the passage. It comes out in the dungeons somewhere."

"Oh," she rejoined, "how long ago did he start ?"

"It must have been three hours or more."

"When we explored it years ago there were pools, the air was bad, and some of the wall was falling. Oh, let us go below at once. Hark ! did you not hear something ?"

They both listened attentively, and presently they heard the sound again as of a dull scraping or knocking. They went quickly below to the dungeons without a word. They traced the sound to a corner which Jean knew well. With Brian's help she removed a stone in the wall, making a hole large enough for a man's body to pass. But beyond, the earth and rock had caved in.

"Quick, a spade or axe," said Brian, for a noise was coming from behind the pile of *débris*.

Jean darted away. Brian called : "Are you there, Bruce ?"

The reply came faintly, "Yes, yes; for God's sake, quick ! I'm stifled !"

Brian laboured at the earth and stones with his hands. Presently Jean arrived with a pick, and an opening was achieved. Bruce's form appeared. He was almost through when he plunged forward insensible. They pulled him out, and, as he did not revive at once, they carried him up to the living-room. Here he recovered and rose to his feet. For a moment he could not quite tell where he was, but when he did he embraced Jean and kissed her. She dropt her head on his shoulder and burst into tears.

They were placed between the lamp and the window in such a fashion that their shadows were thrown upon the blind. A man and woman, standing outside in the yews, saw this, and the woman said: "This is what we've come for, Andrew Venlaw. You saw Brian Kingley enter ; you see that—though it's little thanks I'll get for showin' it you !"

The man caught his breath with a great sob, then he put out his hand towards the woman. "Hush ! In the name of God let me be !" Then, with a cutting breath, "The villain ! the villain ! I'll have his life."

"You'll hae his life, Andrew ? And what right hae you to tak' his life ? She's got her father and brither, and she wasna vowed to you. You'll do nae hurt to the man, for that wad mak' matters waur for her." (Elsie at this moment shrank from the consequences of her deceit). "Confess yorsel'a fule, Andrew ; and be thankfu' ye've escaped ; for the tricks o' beauty like hers arena for men like you."

His eyes were fixed upon the window, but he stretched out his arm again impatiently. "Will ye no cease ? Are you a deevil ?" Then, relenting, "Forgie me, lass; it has made me wild—but gang hame, gang hame, Elsie !"

The beginning of Elsie's punishment had begun. She had to watch the man grieving for this girl, rather than hating her.

"I'll no gang hame wi'out you," she answered. "For ye'll stay here till he comes oot, and there'll be fechtin'. Get you hame and sleep on 't, Andrew, and in the morning ye'll say, as I do, that it's weel to let the thing bide."

He stood for a moment very still, then, without a word, he turned and went through the trees towards the town, she accompanying him. They did not speak until they had neared the still-peopled streets ; then she said to him : "We'll part here, Andrew, for it's no weel that we should be seen thegither at this hour—howe'er careless ithers may be."

The innuendo was plain, but he appeared not to notice it. He turned and grasped her hand. "I believe, Elsie, that ye've tried to be a frien' to me, in this ; and I'll hope never to forget it, though you could hae done mony a service that'd please me better. I'll remember you beyond, lass. Good-bye !"

And he turned abruptly and left her.

She stood still looking after him. "'Beyond—beyond !'" she repeated ; "'I'll remember you beyond ;' thae were his words. Is he going—awa' ?"

"He raised the stone and let it fall into the darkness."

She darted forward as if to speak to him, but he was out of sight.

"Then—then," she said in a low, bitter tone, "he shall have one more blow:" and hurrying, as if determined to give herself no time to change her mind, she went to the Rob Roy inn. She entered the room where Benoni was playing for the dancers. There were several soldiers present, and also two or three officers of the law. She went to one of the soldiers whom she knew, and whispered to him.

"I thought the scamp hadn't gone," he replied. "The subterranean passage is a good dodge, but we'll ham-string him directly." So saying he nodded to Elsie, and went to one of the law-officers present.

Meanwhile, in the Castle, Bruce had explained his plans of escape to Jean. He did not know yet that he was to have company to the Hudson's Bay country. Brian intended that as a surprise for him later. They discussed the probability of the Castle being searched again, for they knew that it was watched. For this Bruce had a plan ready; and if he had immunity from capture for a few days, vigilance would be relaxed, and then he could make his escape more easily to the coast—that is, to Dunbar. His scheme of hiding under the very nose o. the law had so far been daring, but, perhaps, the best that could have been adopted. The policy should be pursued to the bitter or successful end.

Jean had spoken little during the discussion. She did not avoid Brian, but she could not be to him as she had been before, though she tried to prevent Bruce seeing any difference in her manner. As for Brian, he wished to humble himself before her, and would have done so at a certain moment, when Bruce's affairs were arranged in so far as was possible. But she guessed his intention, and warned him with her eyes; and the pleading, suffering, and absolute womanliness of that look followed him for many a year. That chance lost, the opportunity was gone, maybe, for ever. So, with a hasty good-bye, less trying to Jean than it would have been had she known that he also was going over the seas if Bruce escaped, he again gave Bruce the point in the hills where they should meet when he ventured from the Castle, and was gone—out of the girl' life.

Brian had not been gone long when there came a knocking at the door. Jean looked out of the window and saw some dark forms on the Castle steps below. She warned her brother, and they hastily and noiselessly de-scended to the dungeons. Jean did not question Bruce's plans. She had strong faith in his resources. He quickly told her that he was going to hide in the draw-well. He explained that there was a hole in the side of the well, into which a man could crawl, evidently designed for fugitives like himself. Then he urged her away.

She hastily mounted the stairs, and proceeded to open the outer door. The bars clanked down, the panel creaked open, and four men stepped into the light of the candle. Her face showed no excitement, though her eyes were unusually bright.

"What is it you're wantin', men, at this hour?" she asked. "My faither's no at hame."

"Ay, ay, but we didna come to see your faither, lassie, but your brither wha bides wi' ye the nicht, whatever," answered a tall officer.

"Ye'll please to remember that my name is Jean Fordie," the girl responded proudly; "and also ye'll mind that you cam like thieves in the nicht; so be thankfu' that I didna fire on ye, afore asking ye to explain your troublin' the peace of a lonely girl."

"You're vera high and michty, Mistress Jean Fordie, and ye carry your wits wi' you. But I ken that ye're no bidin' alane the nicht. There's places empty at the Rob Roy that should be filled wi' the lilt o' the shoes of Jean Fordie and Bruce Fordie and Brian Kingley, whiles. Oh, ay, there's thochts that 'll be thocht the nicht, whether we wull or no. And so ye'll be just standin' aside, Mistress Jean Fordie, and if yer brither's no here, we'll be findin' wha is here, forbye."

One of the officers had bolted the panel, and stood guard by it. The leader again addressed Jean, since she made no motion forward. "Shall we be takin' the licht frae ye, Jean Fordie, or wull ye gang wi' us and save us trouble?"

Without a word now she preceded them with the light up-stairs; and then every room was searched down to the dungeons. As they were going below the officer said to her: "He'll no have got awa' by ony door syne we've been in, and there's mair o' thae lads outside." He pointed to his companions, and chuckled to himself. The officer, after close search, failed to discover the subterranean passage; for Brian and Bruce had placed the stones again in their proper position, and had filled the interstices with improvised mortar. The officer was baffled. Again they searched the Castle thoroughly, sounding the walls for movable panels, exploring the roofs and the chimneys, and at last coming as before to the dungeons. Suddenly the leader paused at the draw-well. He stooped and lifted the trap-door, and taking the candle from Jean, held it down as far as he could. But it did not light below itself. It is not probable that the man expected to find anything there; he did the thing mechanically. Then he handed the candle back to Jean, turned aside, and picked up a large stone lying loose on the ground. He raised the stone, looking at her. She held her countenance unmoved, but her heart throbbed so violently that she turned sick. He raised the stone and let it drop into the darkness. Jean turned deathly white. As if by accident, she dropped the candle, and it went out. In the gloom they heard the stone boom once, twice, thrice, against the sides of the well; then there was silence, and again a hollow echoing thud as it struck the water.

Then Jean spoke, and her voice seemed, to herself, an infinite distance away. "You see, there's naethin'."

All her life long she thanked God that in that sickening moment she had remembered the hole in the side of the well, else the horrible suspense would have made her shriek out, or restrain the officer's hand.

She heard the trap-door drop. She drew a great breath of thankfulness, and said: "Ye 'll hae to find yer way up again as best you can; or stop here till I get the candle lichted."

They essayed to follow her, however, and groped their way to the staircase and ascended. She hurried up-stairs, lighted another candle, and brought it down to them as they stood at the door ready to go.

"Is there ony ither place you wad care to search?" she said with some sarcasm.

"Ye've a verra canny heid, Mistress Jean Fordie (since ye'll be hacin' the name wi' a' its handles); and ye've helpit him weel awa', I ken. But ye'll no carry that heid heigh in Braithen in days to come, I'll be thinki..'. And that's my blessin' tae ye; which I'd no hae gied ye, war yer tongue no sae sour, Mistress Jean Fordie."

"It's easy for a woman to say bitter things, but it oughtna to be sae easy for a man to answer them bitterly," replied she very gravely, and with a strange sadness in her tone. "And if you had a brither that was hunted like a dog inside his sister's door, ye'd be bitter too, maybe; but ye'd tak' it ill o' onyane sayin' hard things o' thae sister."

There were no tears in her eyes, but they swam through her words. She foresaw all too clearly what the man had prophesied,

though she could not know how far she would be humbled by scandal and falsehood, which was God's tempering of the wind to what she was able to bear. The full strain of her trouble came with her increasing power to endure it.

The officer was taken back by this now attitude. He had been angry at being baffled by a girl; but he knew that his spite was unworthy of a man. He did the manly thing. He said to her: "I'll no say but ye're richt, and I'll be askin' ye to forget what I said tae ye the noo. I'm but a rough carle, ye ken, and ye hae sic an edge tae your words when ye wull. Sae good-nicht tae ye, lassie, good-nicht tae ye kindly."

The door opened, and they were gone.

Meanwhile Andrew Venlaw was sitting alone in his room, his hands clasped between his knees, his eyes fixed painfully upon the floor. Suddenly he raised himself, shook his shoulders as if to free himself of some load, left the house, and went to the Salmon's Head. There he inquired for the Hudson's Bay officer, whom finding he remained with for an hour. When he left again, the other laid a hand upon his shoulder, and said: "Not to Dunbar then, Mr. Venlaw, but London. There straight to me at the address you have, and afterwards—an honest adventurer of the North!"

To this Venlaw nodded an assent, and then strode away into the night, thinking upon his intended exile, but not knowing that those two others were to be exiles to the same regions; and they remained ignorant of his pilgrimage also.

Looking after him, Moore said: "He'll be the very chief of chief factors off there, or I know nothing of the H. B. C. All—all because of a woman. Well, the Company owes much to women. They are the makers of exiles."

Andrew Venlaw twice turned to go to his home, and twice changed his mind. At last he decided, and moved up the river again to Cowrie Castle. When he reached it he stood long in the shadows of the yews. Once or twice a woman's form cast a shadow on the blind; and once a man's shadow was there also. At this, something seemed to disturb him greatly. He shuddered violently. Presently he threw his arms against a tree, and leaned his head on them. If one looked for such a thing of a big man, one had said that he sobbed. But any that had known him years later would have declared this impossible. When he looked up again he said in a shaking voice: "O lassie, lassie, I thocht

ye like the sna'—cauld, but as pure ; and a'
tho time his kisses were burnin' on yer lips.
If I stopped here I maun feeht him, I maun
kill him. But I'm going awa', and I'll forgot
ye by-and-by, maybe. I'll never seek to ken
what's cam to ye ; for the best maun be waur
than this. I'll be gain' frae ye, lassie," he
continued, in tho homely dialect in which he
had been bred, "and nae mair will I look
upo' your face again. Ye hae cursed me wi'
a curse which I'll bear wi' me a' the days o'
my life. For ye hae shaken my faith i' tho
warld—it's true, ay, but it's true—'the
human heart is deceitful abune a' things and
desperately wicked.' Good-bye, Jean Fordie,
and God forgie ye !"

He went slowly back towards the town.
On his way he saw a reveller of the fair
coming. The man was singing a plaintive
ditty in a fashion grotesquely blithe. Andrew
Venlaw recalled it many a time afterwards.
Now it was like blows in the face to him.

> "Nae mair at Logan Kirk will he
> Atween the preachins meet wi' me ;
> Meet wi' me and when 'tis mirk,
> Convoy me hame frae Logan Kirk."

CHAPTER IV.—"THE ICE FIELDS AND
THE MAIN."

Two sister ships are breasting a nasty
Atlantic sea, a hundred miles apart. They
are running, shoulders shivering, against the
wild burglars of the north—the inflexible,
implacable winds. They subtend a great
angle of riot. Above, there is the spiteful
whipping of icy shrouds, the shrieking wrench
of the mast ; below, is the dull booming of
dislodged cargo, the rustling *mélange* of dis-
order. Upon the deck of one of these un-
abashed invaders stands a man remarkable,
even in this buffeting of the elements, for
the strong defiance of a stalwart body and an
indomitable mind ; for an austere firmness
of countenance and stern composure. All
this distinction of character would have appeared possible to one who had rounded the
compass of an adventurous career, but it
seemed hardly fitting to so young a man as
this spectator of a pretty combat between a
little warrior hanging to life by rivets, and
weaponed by cotton, with these tireless co-
horts, ranging the world, waylaying, rattling
the bones of disaster down the corridors of
foam, or again, mercifully breathing new
leases of years into the nostrils of man ;—the
irresistible crusaders of the sea. But age
and character are matters of constitution and
circumstance, and this man had granite in
muscle and mind, drawn, maybe, from a race

of hardy ancestors and the rugged hills of
his native land, as from a sudden collision
of events, whereof we know.

He preferred being lashed to a mast or
capstan to going below. No lurch of the
rowdyish little craft, no racketing of bulwarks, or snapping of spars, or huge onslaught
of the waves dismayed him. He was interested ; that was all. Until he sailed from
London town he had never seen the ocean
nor boarded a big vessel. He was learning
of lands beyond Pentland and seas beyond Forth. He had had as his dream of
the business of life the very pleasant art
of architecture. He had been suddenly
burked of that by a handful of disasters.
Now he was studying the wide architecture of the world along the sluices of the
sea, seizing upon the flying *radii* of the
elements, more ambitious to experience life
itself than to accomplish, merely that he
might say his *Io Triumphe :* which is the beginning of wisdom. He is going to a self-
created exile, but he looks to turn it into
a most brave adventure. It suits him to
grapple with the unexplored and uncompanionable north.

The other ship, which had been a longer
time out on the voyage, was taking her
punishment with a stolid resistance. She
shook off the waves with the big assurance of
old custom, and drove straight along the
trail of her enemies, invincible but creaking
in every joint. She was wounded in a limb
here and there, her bulwarks were splintered
and her sides were clattering, but she ran
her figure-head straight at the bellowing
troops of shipwreck, and held her way. Her
inhabitants, barracked in her well-wedged
ribs, sweltered in the sickening air of her
exhausted lungs, too dull to count hours,
many too timid to leave their tossing beds.
But even here were two men who took the
fortunes of the sea as if they were boon companions of the ship herself, quite as substan-
tially and a deal more gaily. For one had
come out of worse danger than the romp of
the ocean, and the other had left behind a
squandered fortune and a mischievous existence, glad to be rid of harassing consequences, as he was trying to be free of
reproachful memories.

"Listen to that !" said he to his comrade.
"There's the swing of the universe, and the
rebellion of the Poles. Bedad, we're helpless
bits when the elements play tennis with us.
But it's wonderful all the same, tossing about
with the four winds of the world. It makes
a man think. And, my word for it, if I was

a sailor, I'd come to think more about the
Thing behind the storm than the storm itself.
For I'll whisper it to you, my valiant Scot,
the winds and the sea are for the making of
men out of spalpeens, who tread the solid
ground as though there was never lightning
to wither nor water to drown. . . . Are you
listening to the sermon, me boy?"

The speaker laughed softly, but with the
slightest accent of timidity, as if he were not
sure how his remarks would be regarded.
But the other nodded up at him gravely and
companionably, and he went on.

"What's the cause of this, you're askin'
out of your canny eye, Scotsman? . . Well,
lying last night with sleep playing hide-and-
seek round me, I got to thinking of the days
when I was a lad, not so high as the breast
that gave bone to my body, and I thought
of as lovely a woman as ever gave the
world a man, and a day at Malahide where
the sea comes striding in with the pride of
an army, and she saying to me,—"Brian, me
lad, there's nothing on earth so mighty as
the sea and the sun." And she read to me
out of a book like none other—though little
you and I regard it—and made me learn by
heart what she read. And the words came
to me last night, and went swimming back
and forth through my mind. Well, here they
are:

"'The Lord hath his way in the whirlwind and in
the storm, and the clouds are the dust of his feet.
"'He rebuketh the sea, and maketh it dry, and
drieth up the rivers; Babylon languisheth, and Car-
mel, and the flower of Lebanon languisheth.'

"That was the fashion of the thing, and—
Here, take this match for your pipe, and
make never a grin on your face when I say
to you that the word which the good woman
speaks to the child once swung at her
breasts, when she's just stepping out of the
world, is worth keeping better than I've kept
it. . . . But, maybe, my lad of Braithen,
there's a time for remembering everything,
and this is one of them; for, here we are
with a mad record behind us and a walloping
sea beneath us, the wind playing ninepins
with the masts and spars, and a long white
land ahead all snow and wild meat, where
we'll be carrying our lives in the palms of
our hands; and Bruce, me boy——What's
that? . . ."

There was a sudden heaving turmoil beneath them, a harsh horrible shock and grat-
ing, and a big palaver of wind and breakage
above, through which ran the wild cry of a
human voice:

"An iceberg! . . . We're lost! . . ."

. . . . . They were not lost, but a battered,
abused vessel went tumbling on into the
spawn of the elements.

In the room of a gloomy old castle in Scotland, a girl sat at this moment weaving. A
sombre man, brooding at a fireless hearthstone, raised his head now and then as if to
listen to the wind shrieking up from the
courtyard and the ruined chapel to the
quivering window. Several times he took
his pipe from his mouth as if to speak. But
he waited. At last, looking with a sidelong
glance at the grave industrious figure by the
loom, he said: "It'll be bad eneuch for ony
that's travelling the hills the nicht."

"It'll be waur for ony that travels by sea
the nicht," she replied in a far-away, yet
kindly tone.

The old man stirred fretfully in his chair.
"Isna the land eneuch but you must be
fashin' aboot the sea? . . . What's put the
sea into yer head?" he added, something
not quite so gruffly, however.

"Maybe it was God—and my mither," she
responded solemnly.

The old man stared, shook his head as in
protest, and was silent again.

In a cottage on the braeside, at the same
moment, an idiot sat drawing grotesque
figures on the hearthstone with a cinder.
Suddenly he paused, as the rain and wind
spluttered down the chimney upon the fire,
and said with a prodigious leer: "O, O,
whustle, whustle! Puir Else! Puir Pete!
Flee awa'! flee awa'! O wee rats drown!
O, O, Puir Jess! Puir Pete!"

"O, hush, for God's sake, Pete," said a
petulant voice behind him.

CHAPTER V.—THE SLANT OF THE YEARS.

EIGHT years is a considerable measure in
the range of youth. Less time than that has
turned hair grey, brought wrinkles to the face,
dimmed the eyes, robbed a face of blushes or
the power for blushes, and chilled the blood
in the veins. Cowrie Castle looks the same.
Eighty times eight years could make little
difference in it. It stands up grey and tall,
a sentinel among the hills, monumental of
those who had travelled the slant of the
years to where all paths end.

Within the Castle little of itself is changed,
though if you had gone below to the dungeons
you would have seen that the old draw-well
was fastened permanently down, so that none
could raise it. This was one manifestation

of a father's anger when he learned that his son had escaped from the law by its means; perhaps, however, not so much angry at the escape, as at the thing being achieved successfully under his very eye. He had cast the lad out of his heart and home; for he declared he had forfeited the right to one and had dishonoured the other. Yet this lad in his youth had been more to his father than the girl. But that is the way of men: they are often cruelest to those they have loved most.

Black Fordie never inquired after his son. But once every year there came a letter from him to Jean; and she read parts of it aloud as she sat by the fire in her father's presence; but as if she were reading to herself. She knew that he listened, but she never hinted at that. In all else Fordie was kind enough, kinder even than in years past. He was unhappy if she were away for a day. He was moved too by a pity which made him almost tender to her at times. For, since that momentous day of Beltane Fair, Braithen had not been a place of happiness. And Fordie, with impotent anger at the man who had caused her suffering, knew this, as he also knew that she was innocent and good as when she came into the world. Therefore, among the people he was more stern and saturnine than ever. It had been said of Jean that she had loved unwisely a gentleman who left her; and though the tale of Brian's midnight visit to the Castle was explained by those few who were indignant at the injustice they believed was being done to a girl who, maybe, had been indiscreet but not wicked, the matter was persistently kept alive through a source not difficult to trace; and the girl found it hard to live detraction down. Yet she had not lost her beauty. Her face, though less rounded, had the grave sweetness and settled dignity which comes sometimes to the suffering young.

The seventh, the eighth, year saw no letter from Bruce at the usual time. When it was apparent that none would come she visibly suffered. There was no pining look, but her cheek became more delicate, and more sensitive, so that the colour came and went upon it hastily. There was one pleasant thing at the bottom of her Pandora's box. It came year after year, and sometimes twice and thrice a year, in the person of Benoni. She used to wonder why it was she had such a feeling of comradeship for this old man so far below even her social scale. But her father, as if to free her from occasional interrogations, told her once that Benoni was a distant relative, but that she must not question him about it, for there was a story and he wished it to be unknown. Since her trouble had come upon her Benoni had been kind and companionable to her after a new fashion. He came oftener and stayed longer than formerly. He sent her books, most carefully and intelligently chosen; biography, history, romance, old plays, and poets of the time. These had developed her amazingly. Her father wished her to cease weaving, but she would never do so; she would even have gone to the woollen mill, lately established at Glaishen Water, but to this he would not consent at all; for he said, as was true, she had no need to earn her living.

Still, she went to the mill occasionally, because she liked to see the activity of it and to hear and watch the rumbling machinery. Besides, she had a friend there; a pretty girl of merry heart and daring tongue, and who never ceased to sing Jean's praises where most they needed singing; and while the Dominie, her uncle, lived, she constantly and viciously fought him upon the matter of Jean, as upon his attitude towards all women. But Katie Dryhope had one opponent as stealthy as Katie was brave, so that when Jean visited the mill she was received, if not with actual slight, at least with furtive glances, and by no means enthusiastic greeting: due also in some slight degree to the fact that she was superior to them all, both by education and the advantages of breeding got from her mother. But she could and did endure it in a very womanly and proud fashion. She knew her enemy too, for Elsie did not hide the light of her antipathy under a bushel, and always did more than nod significantly when Jean entered the mill.

One summer day, at the point of time when this chapter opens, Jean visited the mill. It was about five o'clock of the afternoon, and the last half-hour of work was on. There was to be a merry-making the following day in honour of an enlargement to the mill, and all the girls were in good humour. The flight of the shuttle was accompanied by a low clatter of conversation. The greeting to Jean was heartier than usual. She turned half unconsciously to the loom where she usually worked, and saw that her place was empty. She was welcomed heartily by Katie, and they chatted pleasantly; but Jean's eyes kept wandering to the deserted loom. Katie saw the wandering glance, and at last said: "She's gane, and for guid; and serve her richt!"

"What serves her richt?" Jean asked.

"That she had to gang, and that she'll no come back. This morning she quarrelled wi' the lassie working the next loom tae her, and she reachit ower and ran a knife clean through the weft. The foreman happened to be goin' by. He see'd it, and awa' she had to gang. He says she'll no get back again, for she was aye making trouble."

"She was a good worker," remarked Jean.

"Of course she was, but that disna matter, and the mill can get alang wi'out her, whiles."

"But can she get alang wi'out the mill, Katie? She has her idiot brother to care for," Jean asked gravely.

"Let her hae a sup o' the misery she's fain to gie ither bodies. It 'ill do her guid," snappishly replied the other.

"Don't be so hard-hearted, Katie."

"You mak me fair angry, Jean," was the impatient rejoinder. "She doesna—love you!"

"But that's no reason for me no bein' sorry for her," Jean urged.

"Oh, you lass!—body, but I could shake ye!" responded the other, her eyes flicking with indignation. She thought that Jean should rejoice at her detractor's downfall. She did actually squeeze Jean's arm till she made her wince with pain. She turned to the loom and muttered detached words of anger for a moment. Then she spoke again to Jean. "Ye're as meek's a moose, and I could sing wi' joy at her goin', forbye."

"I can't forget about the idiot brither, Katie."

"Weel, why doesna she mind that she's gotten an awfu' idiot in the family, and leave ither folk alane, that are saints to her sinner, whiles? Body! I could just break a' the commandments to spite her.—I'll no hear ye speak; I'll no hear ye speak. Ony way ye speak too guid English for me, siccan an education you hae got. There!" And the little warrior laid her hand on Jean's mouth impulsively.

After a little the clacking wheels and pulleys stopped: the soft buzz of the bobbins, the click of the loom, the rattling flight of the shuttles, the thud of weights on the cloth, the swish of the broom over the web, the snip of scissors,—even the smell of the dyeing seemed suddenly to be dissipated,—and the mill emptied into the street.

Jean and Katie passed with the others into the warm air of evening. Never, perhaps, had Braithen appeared more beautiful. Everything glowed. A slight breeze swayed the ancient sign-boards of the burgh, lifted the ivy gently on ruined walls, and swung a stray wisp of hair across the face of a sonsy lass, as she traversed the narrow cobble streets. As Jean and Katie passed down a brae among crying fishwives, lounging soldiers, and some idle revellers, they came suddenly at a turn of the street upon a small crowd gathered round some object upon the ground. Whatever it was it caused the crowd notable amusement, for the girls heard loud laughing as they drew near. They were about to pass the group hurriedly, but Jean, catching sight of the cause of the blockade, suddenly stepped forward among the men, and said with indignation: "Shame on ye, to laugh at what God has deformed!"

Upon the ground sat Pete the idiot, his immense head wagging, tearing to bits raw fish, given him by the coarse humorists about him, and eating it while he laughed horribly. Some drunken fellow had thrown a handful of flour on his head, and another, still more drunken, was offering him a mug of liquor. Jean pushed this aside, and stooping, caught the idiot gently by the arm. "Come wi' me, Pete," she said, "and I'll gie ye better than this to eat, laddie."

The idiot would not stir, but spluttered over his sickening repast. The bright colours of her kerchief caught his eye. He reached out his hand for it. She flushed.

"Come wi' me, laddie," she urged, and she quickly drew the kerchief from her neck and bosom and held it up to him. "I'll gie you this if ye'll come, laddie," she persisted. "Come! do come!"

The idiot tottered to his feet, holding out his hand for the kerchief. She gave it to him and taking his arm led him shuffling from the crowd. Katie had stood a silent spectator of this scene; but when she saw some of the men passing remarks on Jean's palpitating neck and slightly-bared bosom, she turned upon them fiercely.

"Oh, ye raffs and cowards!" she cried. "Ye're grinning at what is a shamefu' thing. For that's Jean Fordie, the best lass i' the borderside and oot o' Heaven itsel'; and as for the fule waddlin', ye're nae better yoursels, when ye're just slobberin' wi' drink. He's what God made him, an' ye're the deil's own wark, an' that 'll awa wi' ye some day tae a place waur ye'll wish ye had been fules like this to be i' Abram's bosom!"

At that a fishwife strode into the crowd and vigorously finished the sermon that Katie so successfully began; and the two

"Whether she likes ye or no!" was the reply, accompanied by a vicious little toss of the head. "She likes ye as weel as I like her, and that's as a cat likes a bird."

But Jean only said: "Ye're harder than you need be, Katie."

They walked on in silence through High Street, and crossed the bridge, causing some remark as they passed—it was not an errand outwardly becoming; but they were brave. At last they entered the street on the brae where Elsie lived. As they did so they saw old Jessie pottering from house to house, protesting with upraised hands that it was not through her fault the laddie had escaped; and that the stroke Elsie gave her on the breast must be repented of in sackcloth and ashes—or something akin to it. "Elsie," she said, "had an awfu' tongue and an unco' sperrit; and nae mair wad she care for the wobbling body, waur nor ony child or ony drunken wabster day in day out wi' his feckless ways. . . . And Elsie," she continued, "was scaurin' the burgh wi' a bit fire on her tongue that micht weel burn Shadrach, Meshach, and Abednego i' ony ... i' Babylon."

She had arrived at this point in her narration, when she noticed Jean

"Old Jessie, protesting with upraised hands."

girls passed down the brae and into High Street with their imbecile companion.

"Whaur 'll you tak' him, Jean?" said Katie.

"I'll take him hame. He has wannered frae auld Jessie that cares for him, and Elsie 'll be in great trouble when she finds he's awa'."

Katie shrugged her delightfully-plump shoulders. "I'd hae left him to eat rotten fish till he was awa' in guid earnest. But if y'ill hae your way, I'll gang wi' ye tae Elsie's house, just to see that she doesna scart yer face for bringin' him back. For she doesna want him, or I'm a fuil mysel'."

"Then you convict yourself, Katie, for she's like a mither to the poor carl, and I'll dae what I think is richt, whether she likes me or no."

and Katie with the truant; while they, in turn, saw Elsie running up the brae behind them. Her black hair streamed behind her, her eyes were flashing with anger. Without a word she ran upon them, caught the idiot by the shoulders, and pushing him in before her to her cottage door, thrust him inside, and entering, slammed the door after her. The only words spoken came from the idiot himself, who cried as he went,—"Puir Else! Oh, oh, the wey flee's drooned—puir Pete!"

The two girls walked away across the river in silence.

After a time Jean said: "Katie, do ye think they wad tak her back at the mill? It's dreadfu' for her."

"She's like a wasp i' the place; besides—oh, I canna bear that you should speak ane word for her, Jean; for she's leed and leed aboot you——"

Jean put her arm through that of the other. "Katie, don't I ken a' aboot that? But the worst o't is ower for me, and a' will come richt some day. I'm no in sic a hurry aboot it noo. Ane gets patient after awhile." Her eyes suddenly swam with tears, but she went on steadily: "I ken, Katie, that the foreman gangs to see your sister Maggie——"

"Oh, Meg leads him sic a dance!" interrupted the little madcap.

"Ay, I ken. Noo, I want ye to mak' Maggie no tae lead him a dance, on condition that he taks Elsie back."

Katie sprang a step ahead of Jean, faced her, caught her by the shoulders and shook her.

"Oh, oh, I could shake you till there's no a shake i' yer body, if yer big een didna look like the picture o' angel's in faither's Bible. But I'll shake ye as lang as I can, whiles, and then——"

Apparently angry, she did shake Jean till she had exhausted herself; then, as suddenly, danced to her side again, and, taking her arm, said: "I'll just do as I please, and that'll be out o' nae love for Elsie Garvan!"

And Jean knew that she had prevailed, and she linked her arm in Katie's, and kissed her on the cheek.

That night Jean had a visitor. She did not expect her father home till late; and while waiting for whoever was expected, she brought out all the letters that Bruce had written her since he had been gone—they were only five—and read them over and over, smoothing them out on her knees afterwards, and thinking about each one before she passed to another. It was scarcely necessary, in one sense, to read them, for she knew them by heart; but the sight of the words seemed to give them new life and character. The last letter had been written from Fort Angel, not very far from the Arctic Circle; and it told of trouble with the Indians, and fierce cold, and hazardous but fascinating hours with wild beasts; and all vibrating with vigour, manliness, and contentment.

After the first two letters Bruce had mentioned Brian only briefly. Their separation, by appointment to different forts, was the cause of this. And men might be for a lifetime in these wilds at the beginning of the century, and not see or hear from each other, so uncertain and roundabout were the mails. In the third letter he said that Brian had left the Hudson's Bay Company's service, and had

"A harsh, horrible shock."

entered that of its great rival, the North West Company. He assigned no reason for this change. After that his knowledge of Brian's whereabouts appeared to cease, though he said he missed his old comrade continually. Bruce had never known of the unhappy event, with its malicious circumstances, which had nearly ruined Jean's life. Brian had never had the courage to tell it; and he did not know what injury he had done.

So far as she knew, no one in the Shiel Valley guessed what had become of Andrew Venlaw. Brian and Bruce were not aware of his presence in the Hudson's Bay Company —for that was part of his compact with Mr. Moore. Only one man in Scotland was certain of his whereabouts, and that was old Dominic Dryhope. For five years Jean was also ignorant on this point, and she thought of Andrew regretfully, because, as time went on, she was sure that he had gone because he had believed ill of her and Brian. At times, too, she thought of this indignantly, but that was while the fresh force of her trial was upon her.

At last the Dominic was taken ill, and Jean went with Katie to see him. At first he would not speak to her, but lay on his couch glowering at her—for had not she ruined his one promising pupil? But as days went on, and her presence affected him, in spite of himself, pleasantly, he unbent to her: and at last he let her and none other tend on him, though he rated her not urgently still.

One day when she came, he appeared desperately exhausted, and presently he told her that he had been finishing a letter to Andrew, begun weeks before. "Ay, lass," said he, "but my bonnie laddie 'll no come back; and sic a heid, sic a heid, he had! An' ye'll no be writin' for him, for ye'll no clap een on him this side o' Domesday; for you've broke the laddie's heart, and a heart can be broke but ance."

For the first time in his presence her bravery forsook her. She sat down beside him, her face pale and drawn with pain. He relented, and pointing to Andrew's picture on the wall, said that she should have it soon, together with the letters written from that far country.

"He wad hae bin a great man, Andy, wasna it that, wasna it that, ye ken!" he said, forgetting, as he came to the end of the long travel, Shakespeare's English, of which he had been so proud.

"I'll no set een on him again; for it's far to yon country, and I'm awa', I'm awa', the noo. It isna caulder there than here the day. Ay, but it's awfu' cauld, it's awfu' cauld i' Braithen. Lass, it's dreedfu' cauld."

Yet it was a summer night, and by that she knew that the end was near. But he demanded again the letter he had written to Andrew, and quill and ink; and with icy fingers he wrote something more upon it, then sealed it, and gave it to Jean, sending her off to the post with it at once. He watched shivering till she returned; and as she entered the door he turned his head to her, and his dim eyes looked out on her from an immeasurable distance. He was seeing her through the infinite glass that stretches between This and That. "Ay, lassie," he said at last, "that's a gran' man. . . . It's awfu' cauld. . . . We're awa'—to the richt."

And she had taken the portrait and the letters, and had carried them to the Castle. And she read the letters through and through, but she found that her name was never mentioned, nor yet Bruce's, nor Brian's. He seemed to have cut himself off from them utterly. Nor did Bruce come to know through Jean of the Dominic's death, and of Andrew's whereabouts; for her letter telling of these things never reached Bruce; and Brian, of course, was less likely to know than Bruce. Only a chance meeting would give Brian knowledge regarding Andrew.

As Jean sat with all these letters before her, musing, her thoughts first and last were with Brian. Though through him had come much of her misery and the harm to her good name, she could not hate him. It was only when the scene on the fair-ground came before her, and she felt again his arm round her, and his lips touch hers—lips wet with wine!—that she shuddered, and shrank away from memory of him. It was a little drama that had been enacted many times these eight years; and it always ended as it did now, by the letters being reverently kissed, and put away behind a secret panel in the room.

Presently she heard a knock, and the one evidently that she expected. She hurried down to the great door and admitted Benoni, who took her hands as the moonlight ranged through upon them, and said: "What, lass Jean, glad to see old Benoni again?"

"I never forget," she replied, closing the door and turning to go up-stairs with him.

"I'm not sure that remembrance is always a virtue," he rejoined meaningly, shaking back his hair, very grey now.

When once inside the room, the showman drew the girl forward to the light. "I must have a good look at you," he said; "to see what the last six months have done to you."

He scrutinized her playfully, and yet with a kind of wistfulness too, and then shook both her hands heartily, and, laughing, asked her if her scones were as fresh as her cheeks. She bustled about to get him some supper. He watched her silent, admiring ; with a look, too, of debate, kindliness, yearning. If ever fatherliness looked out of a man's eyes it did from his.

"Lassie," he said, "what makes you so kind to a vagrant old showman like me?"

"I'm afraid I never thocht o' that. We dinna reason much why we like or dislike. I suppose it is queer your only being a showman, but I think"—here she paused, and gravely looked at him—"I ken that ye maun hae had a different position ance. Just as I always was certain, even afore father told me——"

"What did John Fordie tell you?" interrupted the showman a little sharply, and his face flushing slightly.

"That you were no an Italian, and that you were a verra distant relation o' oors—that's a'!"

"That's all," repeated Benoni musingly ; "ay, that's all!"

"But I can't help thinking——"

"Jean Fordie," interposed the other very gently and solemnly, "I know you think more than you say ; but don't ask me any questions now, and I'll tell you one day, perhaps, who Benoni is, what he is, and why he is."

"I want to say, Benoni," the girl rejoined, her fingers falling lightly on his sleeve, "that even as a showman you, who could do so many great things weel, mak' mony people happy by your goodness."

"As for making people happy, or trying to do so, God gives the poor sometimes, when he grants nought else, two other things— humour and a contented heart ; and I think I have both now, Jean, save in one thing,"

"And what is that ae thing?"

"The thing that troubles you," and the old man's voice was cadenced to a wonderful gentleness.

"Am I troubled?" was her timid reply.

"You have a brother in a country far away ; and two ither—friend.

"Two other friends! What do you mean, Benoni?" She was struggling for composure.

"Two others, as I said. You never told me where Andrew's letters to the Dominie came from ; but I know now where Venla r is. I have seen the Hudson's Bay officer again— the man who helped your brother away."

"Benoni," she urged now a little piteously,

"d'ye ken onything o' them? I haena heard frae Bruce for twa years, as you know."

"I know nothing at all of them, save that the three went there, and they should be here."

"Are the three of them needed?" rejoined the girl a little dryly.

"Two at least should be here, and the brother, if it were safe."

"I do not understand you." This almost in a whisper.

The old man did not immediately reply. He sat down to the supper that had been prepared for him, and began eating, before he said : "When two men wrong a woman, and go away, they should both come back and right the woman, if it cost them their lives and fortunes."

Jean looked at the showman steadily for a moment ; then she glided over to him, and with almost a weird pathos to her tones, said : "Benoni, dae ye think they will ever come—ony o' them?"

There was a long pause. Benoni ceased eating. He turned upon her till her eyes ran direct with his. "If they are alive," he replied, "they shall come back."

"They shall come back?" she questioned musingly, her eyes now apparently engaged with the faded velvet of his coat.

"They shall come back," responded the other more lightly now, and as if a determination had gone into history, "for there's many a worse place than Scotland ; and there's not a better lass in all God's earth than one I know at Cowrie Castle."

A long breath passed from the girl's lips, as though the pain of years had found a moment's ease, and had gone out from her into a comforting world. Then both became silent. When he had finished eating, the showman rose, drew his flute from his pocket, took his accustomed seat at the hearthstone, and began to play. Jean had never heard him play as he did that night : for he appeared to have caught a melody from some Titania and Oberon of a new Midsummer Night's Dream. The gayest fantasies shook through the melody. The dark walls of Cowrie Castle stretched away to interminable, delightful woods, and bright beings of joy danced on the greensward. Then through the exquisite riot she heard a long low note run and rise and rise till it became high and sweet and cold like a bugle call, and go swimming away into the distance, till the shadows of the music ran back and forth in the sky like the Aurora Borealis. While they flickered there Benoni paused, and said with a peculiar smile, "I was calling them back, my dear, from the high shoulders of the world."

Then he poured out another intrepid and penetrating melody, so personal, so immediate, that the girl leaned her head in her arms at the table and sobbed gently. As if the old man was determined that she should have her hour of emotion out, the notes floated into the homely sweetness of *Logan Water*; then running into that joyful call again, he sent it far away till it became a mere film of sound, and so passed away.

He rose and stood beside the girl. "They shall hear those very notes one day, my lass."

She shook her head with smiling sadness. "How shall that be?" she asked.

"I am going to fetch them," the showman drew himself up.

"You—are going—to fetch them?" She was incredulous. "Ye're auld, Benoni; and much money would be needed. Oh, no; ye're no serious."

"But I am quite serious. I am young at heart, and,"—here he smiled in a singular, playful fashion—"and I have money."

At that the girl believed him, and she caught his hand, and kissed it impulsively. Then they sat down and talked long and earnestly together, but were roused by another knocking at the castle door. Jean knew it was not her father's knock. Benoni went below and admitted—Elsie!

"Where is Jean Fordie?" she asked in low excitement.

Benoni guessed that this visit had some unusual significance. He motioned her up the staircase. When Benoni showed her into the room, he would have turned away and left them alone; but Elsie stopped him. "Stay here," she said; "what's to speak is best afore you, for to-morrow I may be richt sorry I tell't it, and ye shall be witness."

Then she turned to Jean. "I'm goin' back tae the mill," she said. "The foreman sends me word that it's through you, it's dune. Ye hae bin guid tae me and mine, an' I hae bin ill to you and yours. You cared for the puir daftie; an' lang syne I made muckle trouble to you."

Then she told her part in that drama of Beltane Fair, 1810, not sparing herself in any particular.

During the recital Jean stood motionless, with flashing eyes. Her face was set and angry. When Elsie had finished, she said: "What made you do it?... I n'ver did you ony harm?"

"You had a'; I had nocht," replied the other, morosely, for the look in Jean's face did not reward her confession with gentleness. "I hated you. Weel?"

Still Jean looked as if she could not understand. "Oh, sic a blind thing ye are!" cried Elsie. "You had Andrew frae me!"

Then Jean understood fully. She drew back from Elsie, a little further as though to see the situation more clearly. At last she said, with amazed and troubled eyes: "You were dreadfu', dreedfu', Elsie!"

Elsie had now to do the hardest thing possible to her nature. She took a step forward and said in a low tone, her bold beauty all humbled before the wronged girl before her,—"Sae sorry am I, Jean Fordie, an' ye hae bin sic a saint!"

Still Jean did not speak. The whole eight years of her suffering went by her in grave procession. She seemed to herself very old: as if she had passed out of the meridian of youth and joy,—though, heaven knows, her face was young and comely still—and the cause of it all was before her. "Oh, Elsie," she said, with a weary kind of indignation, "ye were wicked—wicked!"

"I always wanted Andrew Venlaw . . . I was born with a deevil. That's sae!"

She sat down in a chair, folded her arms before her, and sat flushed and sulky now.

Jean turned and caught Benoni's eye. It suggested nothing; but it turned with a look of compassion on Elsie. Jean went over and laid her hand on Elsie's shoulder. "Elsie," she said; "I hae naething against you. That's over. We will be freens . . . Things canna be altered noo."

Elsie did not stir; she did not look up. But she said slowly: "I wadna hae gane back tae the mill, an't wasna for Pete . . . an ye were sae kind tae him! . . . I hae no sperrit, now. Ye can dae wi' me what ye wull."

Benoni drew away, and occupied himself with his flute. The two talked in a low voice, first, hesitatingly, then freely. At last the showman heard Elsie say "But they'll no come back; it isna ony use."

At this, Benoni rose and came over to the girls. "To-morrow's the merry-making," he said. "After that I'm going to Hudson's Bay—to bring them back."

CHAPTER VI. COUNCILS OF WAR.

A FLOTILLA of boats was proceeding up Red River to the northern lakes which, in turn, connect with Hudson's Bay. Its destination was Fort Gabriel, lying at a north-west angle from Fort Saviour which was governed by Chief Factor Venlaw. The *voyageurs* and *coureurs-des-bois* in these boats were well armed. This seemed necessary, because of peril from Indian tribes. It had, however, another reason. The North West Company, the new and great rival of the most honourable and redoubtable Hudson's Bay Company, was sending this company of men to take and hold Fort Gabriel, a disused but retained post of the Hudson's Bay Company. The object was purely aggressive—a protest against the claims of the Hudson's Bay Company to all the land stretching from the Great Lakes to the North Pole. It was as though China sent a battalion to garrison a fort in Siberia, and held it as disacknowledgment of Russia's claims to the country. The enterprise was not without its dangers, and certainly not without its hardships. It was late summer now, and they must arrive at Fort Gabriel in the water, with the possibility of being countermarched and intercepted by the Hudson's Bay Company, if the object of the expedition should be discovered. But the North West Company had done more. It had sent couriers to certain tribes of Indians in the north and west, promising much, and inciting them to war with the Hudson's Bay Company. It was thought, if the capture of the fort and the uprising of the Indians succeeded, that a crippling blow would be struck at the great Company; so that even if, as had been rumoured, a regiment was sent out from England to sustain the original adventurers and traders, much would be done beforehand to depreciate their influence and claims.

As this flotilla proceeded northwards, it could be seen that the members of the expedition were not taking their matters with desperate seriousness. They were hardy men, if not of great stature, chiefly French half-breeds, swarthy, fancifully dressed, with rings in their ears, like gipsies, and singing much as they journeyed. Time after time these choruses could be heard echoing through the lofty undespoiled woods, startling the elk and the bear from their resting-places, and inviting the wild *yawp* of wolves in the moonlight. Among many this was most frequent:—

> " Il y a longtemps que je t'aime,
> Jamais je ne t'oublie.— '

Once, in the early morning, as they rowed gaily away to the lilt of the blackbird's song, themselves singing the famous—

> " Sur la feuille ron—don—don—lon,
> Sur la joli' joli' feuille ronde,"

the rearmost *voyageurs* were astonished to hear the refrain caught up distantly by some one playing an instrument in the thick woods upon the bank. They were, however, going swiftly, there were reasons why they should not unnecessarily encounter (possibly) a detachment of Hudson's Bay Company men, and they left the music rapidly behind them. The leader of this expedition had, however, caught the faint echo of this music, and for an instant a strange, suggestive smile played upon his face; then it changed to incredulous amusement, and he shook his head at himself. " Faith, it was uncommon like the old showman's flute. A trick of the fancy though; and, bedad, flutes are more or less alike, for that matter ! "

It was Brian Kingley, late of the Hudson's Bay Company; at present, of the North West Company. Brian's record with the company under whom he first adventured had been creditable up to a certain point. Then separation from Bruce came, then loneliness of a sombre kind to an impressionable vivacious nature like his. He was beginning to live with a memory, and that is a most wholesome thing when it concerns a good woman. But the solitariness of one winter overcame him, so that he fell a victim to the rum stored in the fort. His case came to the Governor. Before it was decided he resigned. He made a journey to see Bruce, but the latter had been ordered to another post, and he missed him. Then he went south, made his way slowly, soberly, to Montreal, and became an officer of the North West Company, rising out of all precedent, and now chosen for this hazardous and important task. He conquered his weakness ; he started anew ; he was proving himself worthy of a worthy memory. He had the faculty for getting the utmost out of his men, with the least expenditure of effort and command. True, he had been known to knock down a recalcitrant half-breed, but that was neither injurious to his reputation nor his influence. They had no hardships which he did not share ; his food—simple enough in most cases—was their food ; and he had been known to give the last cubic inch of his pemmican to a starving Indian. His heart was not entirely in this enterprise ; still, he believed, as became an officer on duty, t. at the Hudson's Bay Company claimed too much, and that the North West Company, or any other company, should be free to trade in all the lands of the north. He did not relish the enterprise, because he had once been an officer—a not unimpeachable officer —of the Hudson's Bay Company. But the strain of adventurous blood was strong in his veins, and he enjoyed the excitement and hazard of the affair. So he kept his men encouraged and nerved to the expedition by his own activity and cheerfulness, and they travelled on.

Another expedition from Montreal had preceded his. Its leader was a grey-haired man with a foreign name, who, however, spoke English fluently, and from the chief agent of the Hudson's Bay Company in Montreal had got accurate information regarding two officers of the company—a third, he learned, had joined the rival company, but his whereabouts he could not discover. He travelled westward with a small company of *voyageurs* of the Hudson's Bay Company, but left them at a certain point on the Red River, and, thenceforward, travelled with a half-breed and an Indian whom he paid to accompany him. The flotilla commanded by Brian Kingley passed him one morning, as he lay helpless in his tent from an injured leg, and as both the Indian and the half-breed were away hunting at the time, he could give a sign of his existence only by the call from his flute. But, as we know, the flotilla passed on . . . and so is fate ironical sometimes.

As we have hinted elsewhere, Bruce and Brian did not know of Andrew's presence in the country; and if the name of the chief factor at Fort Saviour—known by the Indians and half-breeds as Ironheart—reached them in later years, they did not associate it with the ambitious youth of Braithen. But it was he. Venlaw had risen by stages extraordinary to the position of chief factor, partly by reason of his unusual influence upon the Indians, because he had impressed himself upon the Governor, on a visit the latter had paid to the most northern posts and forts, and lastly, because he was a substantial success in everything that he attempted. Fortune seemed always to be with him. His enemies as his friends were given over into his hands. That is, where his friends—or *confrères*, rather, for he had no friends, strictly speaking—missed good-luck, it came beseechingly to his hands. The furs he sent from Fort Saviour were double those sent from any other trading-post in the north. He feared nothing; he bent to nothing; he challenged everything, but without bravado. If he was not absolutely loved, he was entirely respected, and always and in everything obeyed. His

advice had great influence with the Council of the Company. The only time it went for nothing was when he suggested the retention of Brian Kingley in the service. (He knew of Kingley's presence in the North: but Kingley knew nothing of him.) This the Council could not understand, for Venlaw was, generally speaking, a rigid disciplinarian. However, on the emphatic protest of Mr. Ashley Moore, their trusted agent, who arrived subsequent to the occurrence, they offered to reinstate Brian; but this Brian refused.

It was Ironheart who, when a certain tribe were threatening, used all instant means to conciliation, making, at the same time, preparations for a struggle, and, failing placable negotiations, administered a prompt and crushing punishment, himself leading his ha̅ndf̅ul of men excellently armed. He bro̅u̅g̅ht the chief to the fort, treated him we̅l̅l y̅et firmly, secured terms of peace on behalf of his tribe, and gained their alliance and powerful advocacy in dealing with other tribes. The Indians of the Sun Rock, with their chief, Eagle Cry, he had also placated, and these had made their village not far from Fort Saviour.

Bruce's promotion, Venlaw had from a distance secretly and not unsuccessfully urged on occasion. Brian he watched; that was all. It was declared in the Hudson's Bay country that this chief factor was a good waiter, and there is a saying in the land to-day, which was current in his time, concerning his masterful perseverance, his sober "staying" power, and his strength. It runs: "As the clinch o' Venlaw." He was absolute in his determination that every man should do his duty; he was tireless himself. Unlike many of the factors he had not taken a wife from among the Indian women, nor had he, as others had done, sent to England for a wife, and received her, invoiced, maybe, like any other careful cargo. He was very stern also with his subordinates regarding their relations with the heathen women. Yet, while in most matters perspicuous, he failed to see what every one else at the fort saw, that Summer Hair, the daughter of Eagle Cry, regarded him with an admiring eye. Had he been told of the fact he would probably have been incredulous, for he was not a vain man. Besides, it would have caused him some anxiety, for the matter would have its difficulties.

The Chief Factor would have been surprised had he been told that he nourished vengeance; he would have called it justice.

To most of the world his disposition was kind, but to two people he had a constant hardening of heart. One of them was Brian Kingley, the other was. Elsie Garvan. We are inclined to cherish dislike, not only against the criminal who wrongs us, but against the informer also. He had actually tried to do Brian a good turn, but the exact motives would be hard to trace. Perhaps he hoped to get him into his power if he remained with the Company, and some day might be able to strike him a terrible blow. As it was, he was sure that Heaven would give the man into his hands. And he would punish, as was granted to him, firmly, unimpulsively, thoroughly. His view of life was justice — unquenchable, unchangeable, unyielding; he loved justice, maybe, more than mercy. He was prepared to endure whatever came to him through his own fault, he was sure that others should do the same. He did not give himself credit for any genial softness of nature; he thought himself more inflexible than he really was.

After nine years of waiting, he knew that the beginning of his reckoning with the past had come. For, one day, there came across the country from the Saskatchewan valley to Fort Saviour a man who bore messages concerning an uprising among the Indians—the uprising projected by the North West Company, who had not acted as secretly as they had hoped to do. This man came to the fort with only a handful of his followers, having made a perilous journey through cold and ambush. When he and his men arrived he was ushered into the fort greatly exhausted, and subsequently was brought to the Chief Factor, for whom he carried messages. When he entered the room the Factor was giving some instructions to his clerk, and did not look up at once. Presently the new-comer, with a start and exclamation, took a step forward. Then the Factor turned and saw the astonished face of Bruce Fordie!

The Factor was not so surprised as his visitor, though he had not suspected who it was. Although Bruce bore communications to Chief Factor Venlaw, he had no thought that it might be Andrew, for the name was not an unfamiliar one among Scotsmen, and the Hudson's Bay Company was honoured by the presence of many of that nationality.

"Andrew Venlaw!" said Bruce, when he could speak free from amazement. The Chief Factor motioned his clerk from the room.

"I did not expect to see you, Bruce Fordie, though I knew that we should meet one day," he said. His eyes ranged steadily to those of his visitor, and not without a sturdy cordiality, for did he not look into eyes like that of the one woman ?—— though!

"What brought you here, Andrew ?"

Venlaw laid his hand on the other's shoulder. "There are two kinds of exiles, Fordie : those who do wrong and those who are wronged : both are here."

They sat down.

"Who wronged you, Venlaw ?" This, in itself, was a somewhat direct compliment, though it was Fordie's spontaneous thought.

"I'll bring you face to face with him one day, Fordie. . . . But now there's business to do first. What brings you here ?" He drew himself together as though he had shaken off, for a moment, some unpleasant thought.

"News for the Chief Factor."

"Well ? . . . Let me have it."

Bruce had almost forgotten that the Chief Factor was before him; he had only been talking to Andrew Venlaw, his old fellow-citizen. But the officer in him reasserted itself immediately, and he gave to Venlaw his letters and such verbal information regarding the uprising as was not in them. His most important verbal information was got en route through a deserter from Brian Kingley's detachment, who had been punished for insubordination, and had, on the first opportunity, thrown in his lot with a straying band of Indians. It related to the capture and garrisoning of Fort Gabriel.

"And you'll be surprised and sorry enough, I know," said Bruce, "when I tell you that the leader of this expedition is our old comrade, Brian Kingley."

Venlaw started to his feet. A singular look came over his face, a smile at once meaning and bitter. "It is Brian Kingley, is it ?" he said. Then, looking Bruce in the eyes with a flash of irony, he continued: "You and I will be glad of this, Fordie !"

"Indeed, I don't see that, Venlaw—far from it. For Kingley was the best friend ever I had, and helped me at a time when the luck was black against me."

"Indeed ! But do you know, man, the price you paid for that friendship ? You got your life and freedom, but there are things more than life and freedom." He was gloomy and stern now.

"I know the price I paid, though, maybe, by your looks, not the price that's in your mind. I know that when he left the H.B.C. the heart went out of me."

"We will be freens."

"He was a drunkard, and worse," rejoined the other sharply.

"You needn't speak so bitter of my friend, Venlaw," replied Bruce, nettled, and unheeding that he had a superior officer in front of him. "You always had a particularly fine record with the dominie and the kirk, we all know, and was a bit jealous and overbearing too. P. Brian Kingley never did you any harm, so why should you speak so of one that came from the same burgh, Irishman though he is?"

Venlaw's words were like cold steel now. "Nevertheless, I shall be glad of the chance to fight him, and so shall you, Fordie."

"So shall I never be. I'd cut off my hand first. I'd no more march against Fort Gabriel than against the grave of my mother."

"In God's name, hush, you fool!" cried the other, the veins starting out on his forehead. "What you think of me, I care not, for I know you thought little of me at any time; but, by heaven! you shall not mention him and your mother in the same breath of kindness."

"You talk about the price I paid for Brian's help in getting out of Scotland, and now you stop me again when I say my mind," replied Bruce. "Well, speak out like a man, Venlaw, and not hint through the dark. And, before you do, I'll say again in your face as man to man and not as a junior to senior officer, that I'd leave the Company were I you, before I'd draw sword upon one that slept between the same hills, and had days of youth to the sound of the same river. And as for me, I'd fight with him before I'd fight against him. And there's my say, if it isn't pleasant to you nor to me, meeting after a run of years."

Venlaw was very hard and deliberate now. His mood was inexorable. He had his mind clear. He was right he knew; justice was right; revenge was right; retribution was right. He said calmly: "Fordie, I've much to tell you about this, and about this man. But your coming was sudden, and I am not ready on the instant to say all that is necessary. You've had nothing to eat since you came. Go and eat, my friend, then come back to me here, and we shall talk together like men. If, when I've had my say, you still retain your opinion for him and against me, then, I swear to you, neither I nor my men shall fight him. You shall judge between us, and I shall judge between you!"

He called his clerk, and, with a nod, Fordie, not yet soothed, turned to go. But he paused before he went, and said: "I'm sorry to quarrel with you at all, Andrew, for I canna forget that we hae both ben lads in a bonnie land lang syne."

Andrew, in reply, only said in the same homely dialect: "You needna forget it, Fordie, and you'll know soon the difference between the hand o' a brither Scot and brither townsman, and that of an alien."

Bruce shook his head gloomily and left the room.

When he had gone Venlaw sat down at his desk, and took out a packet of letters. He laid them on the desk before him and looked long at them. At last he took one up and opened it. It was from old Dominie Dryhope, as were they all. This one was the last that the Dominie had written to him. And the body of it ran :—

"Ay, laddie, Scotland is a cold country. But it's colder now you're gone. There are many men and women in the world, but you'll find as you get more in years that there are few who put life in old bones, or flourish the warmth in young ones. And I'll warrant you wish I was with you now, old as I am, for we were good comrades one time, and there is nothing selfish or jealous in the love of an old man who is done with vanities.

"All that you have written of grand days in that north country, with bullets for buffalo, and bear, and deer, and some sharp play with the arrows and tomahawks of copperskins, I've read over and over again; for that's what will be puttin' mair iron intil your blude, laddie. Aye, you ken, I fly off from my English now and then and just take to the bonnie Scotch, though Shakespeare was a gran' man, forbye! An' the huntin' and the fightin' are better than takin' the fause bosom o' a woman to yours, laddie. . . I canna blame you for goin' awa' syne she wreckit your life, so that ye flingit ambition i' the dust—an sic a gran' ambition was it ! . . . But it hasna ben the same i' Braithen, whiles.

"An' as for the lass hersel, they speak ill enough of her the noo, that turned a willin' ear to the tongue of that Irish wabster, wha played fause a' round, baitin' the brither to spoil the sister. . . Aye, man, but that waur the deil's trap.

"They'll be forgettin' you here, Andy, for that's the way o' the warld; all but the old Dominie, that's graspin' the skirt o' life wi' a shakin' hand, and that'll never see you again i' the warld— never mair !

"I've no given to ony body where you are, laddie, as you begged, and for that I'll doubt if you'll know to the day when I'm awa'. But this'll be the last letter I'll be writin' to you. For the auld body goes quakin' by its grave the noo. But you'll come back, Andy, and see that my wee house i' the kirkyard isna level wi' the groun'. And, ye ken, if they havna put a line abune the stone, you'll be puttin' there i' the corner—'For His mercy endureth for ever.' . . . And what is mine o' house and land, little though it be, is yours wi' my blessin'. For I'll leave naething to the bit lasses that ca' theirsels by my name i' the toon, ilka ane o' them as fause as a' the kin o' woman !"

To this letter appeared a postscript, written weeks later, the occasion of which we know. This is the fashion of it :—

"That lass o' Fordie's has ben here, Andy, day in day out, as I keep crumblin' to the dust ; and though I spoke bit harsh to her, I couldna feel but kindly, for she hae the way o' gentleness wi' her ; an' sic beauty has she still ! An', maybe, she didna go sae far wrang as was tellt o' her, for that Elsie's a jade, Andy ! . . . And you'll no deal wi' the man till you're sure. But if you are sure, deal wi' him as the Lord wi' the children o' Midian.

"The breath o' me gaes waly, but it isna sae bad. . . . Ay, but it's comin' like sleep . . . blessed be God . . . !"

The Factor sat thinking long. Upon the small window of the room snow was beating. He stood up and looked out. Nothing could be seen except the wall of the fort, and an occasional figure, wreathed in snow like a ghost, passing and repassing between. Then, the snow deepened further, and there was nothing but a white curtain hung between him and the world. There came to his mind a day far back, when he had started to bring Jean from his father's house in the glen to the Castle ; and a storm fell suddenly, growing till it became almost a blinding sheet, and they were near to dying, for they lost the way. But he held his arm about her, and kept her as warm as he could, urging her passionately and successfully to keep awake, and not give up. And he had often said to himself, in thinking upon this, that had she been less brave and strong of will than she was, she had been seen no more alive in Braithen. But she was of uncommon

quality, and together they stumbled into
Braither, horribly numb and sick, but were
brought back to life and comfort again.

He shuddered to think how different it
stood in his memory now. Once it was part
of her; now she was only part of it. He
would give the best of his life to think
of her without pain, as he used to do. . . .
Through his mind, at times, there ran the
possibility of there having been some mistake,
some bitter mistake. But then, that scene
on the fair-ground, when she did not rebuke
Brian by so much as a look even! No, the
thing was all too shamefully clear. Yet he
had no anger against her; he had only inex-
tinguishable pain, and hatred of the man who
had wronged her. Perhaps it had been nobler
had he stayed in Scotland; but then he did
not know that Brian was coming to the New
World, and he merely fled from misery, and
from shame and fighting, and to forget . . . .
Still, there was the old Dominie's letter even
saying a good word for her, and this was the
last convert he could have expected, so hard
had he always been against her. . . . But
no; he or Bruce, or both, should dig the
truth out of Brian's body soon. He would
not hesitate to make the Irishman eat the
bread of retribution and the sword.

Presently Bruce entered. His face was
troubled. The Factor's words had rankled.
He thought they might have a deeper meaning than at first appeared to him.

"And now, Andrew Venlaw, I'm ready to
hear all you have to speak," he said, sitting
down beside the table, and folding his arms
on it.

"As I said," slowly spoke the Factor;
"Brian Kingley is your enemy and mine.
When he was helping you from Scotland he
was doing you (and me) harm—in another
way."

Bruce made a gesture of impatience. "I
want the heart of the thing," he interposed.

Venlaw drew the letter from his pocket.
"You'll know the man who wrote this,
Bruce—the Dominie. He's dead now. He
was a good friend to me. Read the letter
through before you speak to me." And he
handed it over.

Bruce read the letter at first slowly. Then,
suddenly, a great flush sprang to his face, and
he devoured the remainder of the writing
with staring eyes and distressful features.
He came fiercely to his feet, and the letter
dropped from his fingers upon the table. His
hand clenched the hunter's knife in his belt.

"Venlaw," he said, with a great hardness
in his tone, "tell me all you have to say of
my sister and yourself, and of that man. . . .
And speak no word but what you would be
willing to say at God's judgment; for there
are big accounts to settle, and stern things
to do."

Both standing, scarcely moving, the Factor
told Bruce the story of the fair-ground.

"He did that—drunk—before them all!"
interrupted Bruce. "I shall take return for
it with a knife-point." Then, after a moment, shuddering, "You know of more, yourself?"

Venlaw bowed his head.

"What you have seen with your own
eyes?" bitterly asked the bruised and venge-
ful man.

"Yes, God help me! with my own eyes,"
answered the Factor, thinking of that night
when he saw Brian enter the castle, and the
embracing figures subsequently upon the
blind. He sat down and dropped his forehead on his clenched fists.

"Don't speak it then, Venlaw; don't speak
it. For I know you loved her, and what
you say is wrung from you. It would be
knives in my heart to hear more."

It would have saved them both much suffering, and events would have marshalled to a
prompter, happier conclusion, if the Factor
had spoken; for Bruce had then instantly
swept away that evidence against Jean.
From such slight circumstances have the
darkest tragedies of the world been spun.
In this case, however, light, not darkness,
should ultimately supervene.

"Venlaw," continued Bruce, "this man's
life is mine and yours; but mine first. I'll
go with you to Fort Gabriel."

The Factor shook his head. "No, you
cannot do that. Your orders were to return to
Fort Mary, bearing my instructions and sug-
gestions on the campaign. Duty must be
done. Fort Gabriel must be recaptured, if
it has been taken, and the Indians of the
White Hand must be defeated by means of
a conjunction of our forces—but the Fort
before that!"

Bruce paced the floor excitedly. "It is
my duty as an officer to go back to Fort
Mary, but there's the duty of a man to do."

"No, Fordie, you must go back; for there
are lives at stake. Afterwards you can settle
private debts like these. There will come a
time!"

Suddenly Bruce wheeled, and with hands
resting on the table before him, and eyes
steadying to the other's, said: "Venlaw, the
man must die. I would give him no chance of
escape at all. For, as much as a man once was

your friend, and abused that friendship, so much must you be his enemy and punish."

The Factor nodded.

"Well, you will meet him at Fort Gabriel. If you make him prisoner, or he gets away, he may escape for ever. Heavens! my blood boils when I think how I made a comrade of the traitor—and that wickedness in him all the time! Then this, Andrew Venlaw:—I lay it upon you, as solemn as the words of a dying comrade—that you fight him man to man when you find him, and kill him . . . kill him!"

Venlaw rose, reached out his hand to the other, and with a harsh smile and an inflexible determination, said : "I will kill him!"

CHAPTER VII.—A COURIER OF SAFETY.

The Factor and Bruce Fordie had arranged for the settlement of a private wrong, but there were public wrongs to circumvent. To these the Factor bent his mind. Soon after his notable interview with Bruce, he set forth upon a solitary mission to Eagle Cry and his Indians. It was necessary, in any trouble with the Indians of the White Hand, that these should be with him in friendly compact, if not as actual fighting allies. Yet he had a shrewd suspicion that they would be receiving emissaries from the hostile tribes or the North West Company, and his influence must immediately be thrown into the scale. It was his way to grapple with difficulties alone. That was what made his counsel of value to the company so often : why the Factor of Fort Mary sent to him now, requesting him to arrange the plan of action, while he and his people would follow and coincide to the best of their ability.

These difficulties always nerved Venlaw. His brain was not swift, but when it was roused it was massive, and worked massively. The influence of the north had developed all the latent power in him ; he himself never saw anything inappropriate in his alternative name, Ironheart. He smiled at it a little grimly ; that was all. Then he thought as few men placed in his position in these cold regions did. The north had not dulled his mental activity, but enlarged it, made it tenacious. It is awesome to a mind of any depth, to live alone much where Nature is immense and terrible. It takes on greatly of her grim force as of her huge joy. A man in the stupendous North either becomes a pigmy or a worm unregardable, a giant or companion of the great giant, or a mere track upon the snows, to be covered immediately by another snow. A man should bulk according to the greatness of the lever which he grasps.

Venlaw was as much a part of the Arctic regions as if he had been born with them and grown with them since they rose out of fire and chaos. His God was the God of the wanderers in the desert of Sin ; magnificent, personal, inflexibly just. Venlaw had been slow to anger. He had been in no hurry for vengeance. It is in hot lands where passion is violent—and grotesque.

As he walked away across the plains, on which snow was still falling slightly, his mind, after thinking hard upon the event wished for at Fort Gabriel, gave itself up solely to the question of Eagle Cry and his intended interview. He scarcely knew what was going on around him ; he kept his way mechanically. He came to the outskirts of pine woods. This interrupted his thoughts. He looked up. The sun was now shining brightly. He leaned against a tree and glanced back along the way he had come. Far on the edge of the plain was the Fort, a solemn spot in the horizon. He was roused by the light pad of snow-shoes behind him. He turned and saw a pair of large brown eyes looking into his, out of a tawny face which glowed also with the most delicate under-hue of red. They belonged to an Indian girl, not beautiful as white women reckon beauty, but with amazing grace and lissomness, and very comely altogether. She wore a long dress of buckskin beautifully ornamented, a coat and *capote* of the same, and her small feet, cased in pretty moccasins, carried snow-shoes as a nymph might. She drew off a mitten, and frankly reaching out her hand to the Factor, said : "The storm is gone and you come with the sun, Ironheart."

He smiled gravely. "Summer-Hair," he said, "how do you come here?"

She looked demurely down at her snow-shoes, then up into his eyes, and waved her arm playfully through the air. "The birds fly, the wild goose swims on the wind, and Summer-Hair rides as they ride." Here her look became mischievous. "They think I walk on these," she added, looking at her snow-shoes, "but I don't ; I walk as the clouds walk."

"I almost believe you do," was his reply. "For you come out of nowhere, and when one least expects you."

Her young face grew for an instant grave, then she looked at him shyly. "That is the way with me. I know when you are coming, and where you are." Then her shyness ran into playfulness again. "For, you see, I am

so much with the clouds, and can look down."
Her fingers tossed fantastically upwards.
"Yes, and I know whether you will be dark
like thunder or as the still water that shines
in the sun. . . . You are like the thunder
now, and I am here. . . . I am not Summer-
Hair. I am a spirit." She clapped her
hands gently before her, then spread them
out in the sun with a gesture of delight: an
Ariel of the north, yet an Ariel with a wistfulness too.

To any other man this would have been
bewitching to a degree, for, when Summer-
Hair's face lighted up, as dark faces can light,
eloquently, when there ran into it the pulse
of the brilliant short-lived summer of the
north, whose brightness she seemed to have
stolen, she was charming. White men at
Fort Saviour had tried to win her for a
wife, but she had put them off, nor had she
been wooed successfully by one of her own
race. Most of the young men of the tribe
had, in fact, come to look upon her as impossible to them, though Eagle Cry had in time
commanded and beseeched, and the young
braves had entreated. Once a brave from a
neighbouring tribe had her father's consent,
and came, determined to carry her off bodily,
but gently as a lover should. She had, however, shown a sudden and complete resistance, as inclement as it was formidable, for
her arrows were well pointed, and the knife
in her belt was of good metal. So the Indian
went back to his people, discomfited. But
another Indian of her own tribe, by name
Red Fire, had appeared of late, from the
ranks of the rejected, and he was playing
his game of love with an astonishing per-
tinacity. With the Chief Factor Summer-
Hair was, as we have seen, very companionable.

"You are going to see my father," she
abruptly said. She asked no question; she
made a statement.

"Yes. Is he at his lodge?"

"He is at the council-house with the
braves," she replied. "There is a big talk.
Runners have come from the far west—from
the White Hands. There is much trouble,
and the young braves are excited."

Venlaw nodded. "Ah, I expected that.
The Merchant Company and their allies are
playing a deep game. But we shall see. . . .
Your father—what of him?"

"He is old, and the young men talk
loudly. He, as I, was sure that you would
come."

"I will go on to him now," said the Factor;
and he stepped out

"Wait," she said. "Are you not afraid?"
Again mischief looked out of her eyes.

"Afraid," he replied, his voice ringing a
little, "of Eagle Cry and his braves? They
are my friends. . . . Besides . . . !"

"But wait," she urged, as she saw him
again turn to go. A singular smile played
upon her lips. "Do not go by the old post-
house, for the young men of the White Hands
are there. They are drunk with rum, and
drunken men strike from behind."

He raised his eyebrows at her, then said
coolly: "I will not go by the old post-house,
then."

Once again he made as if to leave her, and
still again she said, "Wait." Her face was
now a little cold; there was no demureness
in her eyes. One foot tapped the ground
viciously. "You have not thanked me, Ironheart?"

He turned now and looked at her steadily.
His great face flushed to the brim of his fur
cap. His hand fell upon his beard with an
embarrassed gesture. "Summer-Hair," he
said, his voice telling with honesty, "I am
an awkward fellow, and very selfish, and I
think more always than I speak. I ought to
have spoken here. That was unmannerly.
But I have so long counted you a friend and
ally of the Company that I did not consider
you are a woman too."

"I am your friend and ally, Ironheart,"
she rejoined, "but I am a woman too, and—"
here she looked up at him with a swift but
pretty irony—"a woman needs to be thanked."

"Will you forgive me, Summer-Hair?" he
said bluntly, and with a manner as would be
natural towards a child.

She caught the tone, and it drew her up,
looking anger at him, but instantly that
changed, and the better reasoning prevailed,
that even the great Ironheart was only a stupid
man, and could not and did not understand
even an Indian woman. Then, too, she recalled to herself that she did not quite wish
to be understood, and she said, with an
assumed indifference, which had not been
discreditable to a gifted sister-woman of
another sphere and hemisphere,—"There's
nothing to forgive, Ironheart. I was teasing
you. . . . I am only a child," she added,
with the faintest sarcasm. Then she grew
grave immediately, and said, with warning
in her voice: "Let Ironheart be careful how
he talks with Red Fire. The Indian has,
sometimes, a forked tongue."

"Summer-Hair," he responded with enthu-
siasm, "you're the best friend to——"

"I'm the best friend in the world," she

interjected, with archness of voice and manner, and waving her hand to him she sped away, an agile swaying figure, into the woods.

He stood and thought a moment, then walked slowly on, once or twice shaking his head doubtfully, and looking back towards the spot where he had last seen her. She had done the same with a difference. She arrived at the Indian village long before he did, for she had travelled with much swiftness, and had taken a shorter way. She found the braves still gathered in the council-house. The great room of the tent was partitioned by a curtain, and behind this she placed herself that she might hear all that was said. She feared that some untoward decision should be arrived at before Iron-heart came. Some had spoken bitterly of the palefaces in general, and had declared for union with the tribes of the west, and a war against the great companies; others had proposed simply the spoiling of Fort Saviour and Fort Mary; but the old men had counselled peace and amity. Of these was the chief, Eagle Cry. The young men were led by Red Fire. The latter, with biting arguments, opposed their chief. Theoretically the opposition of the Indians to the white invaders was unassailable. The Hudson's Bay Company and the North West Company were conquerors and spoilers.

The secret of Red Fire's strong antagonism could be traced in the insinuating remarks made to Eagle Cry concerning Summer-Hair. At last he boldly declared that his chief's counsels for peace were influenced by the fact that he wished to make his daughter the wife of the white sagamore, Ironheart. At this Eagle Cry rose, as if in final speech for the reply. He said: "Brothers and warriors, I have been a chief of the Sun Rocks for forty years. I took no wife, I had no children till I had begun to see the shadows fall towards the east. My heart was big with war, and we fought many tribes, conquering, and some here are of the conquered, now one with us. Then came a time of peace. In those days my wigwam was lonely, and I took a wife from the daughters of the Flying Clouds, the sacred race. There was joy among the Sun Rocks, many fires were lighted, and there was long feasting. We prospered. As we had been victorious in war, we were perfect in peace, and the land was filled with plenty. The snows fell not so heavily and the north winds had mercy. My marriage pleased the High Spirit. So we continued. We became allies of the Great Company. And we have re-

mained so. But, for the child: She grew up among you. She loved you all as brothers and fathers. She was kind to the sick, and cared for those whose kinsmen fell in the forest through sickness, or death by wild beasts. Her mother died one day when she was yet a little child. Her tribe was her mother. She has been the pride of her tribe and of her father's lodge to this hour."

Here the old man paused, and stood stately and thoughtful. There were long murmurs of approbation from the older men, and the young men were silent, but they had now no anger in their faces.

"Then came the time when she should take a husband. The young men presented themselves. She loved them as brothers. She was kind to them; but she had no love as the wife loves, and she would not go with them. There was one brave whom I wished for her. I said to him "Come," and he came. But he was quick of temper and impatient, and she sent him away lonely. Well, his heart is angry because of this—this man whom I desired. He is angry with me and with the Great Company."

Again he paused, and there was absolute silence, save where the breath of Red Fire came weightily.

Eagle Cry continued: "It was the Great Company that saved us when the terrible sickness fell, and our people faded like the leaves before the October wind. Ironheart has been our friend. He has taught us many things; he has traded fairly with us; he has kept his word; he has sat in our lodges and has been a comrade with us. . . . He is a brother, but no lover of Summer-Hair. I do not want him for a son; he does not want me for a father. Let us be at peace. My heart is friendly towards Red Fire, but he speaks wildly."

Here the old chief drew himself up to his full height, and folded his arms across his breast. "Eagle Cry wishes to be as a brother to Red Fire, but there must be no crooked speaking, for though your chief is old, he is chief; he has wisdom, and he is without fear."

He sat down amid a murmur of approbation.

Red Fire looked round, and scanned the faces of the braves. He saw that his counsel for war had been overborne, and that the chief's speech had lost him much. He was vain and passionate. He grew very angry and rose to his feet. He was about to speak, when the door of the council-house opened, and Ironheart came in among them. He looked round calmly. "My brothers of the Sun Rocks," he said, "I have come to share your counsels. Red Fire, who is of the bravest among you, is about to speak, but I would greet him, before his words of wisdom go forth to us;" and he stretched out his hand. The two men looked at each other steadily for a moment. It was a case of superior will and force. Red Fire was fierce and vain, but he had strength. Vanity and strength saves even an Indian from the treacherous thing. There was a moment of suspense. The indomitable sincerity and character of Ironheart conquered. But Red Fire folded his arms over his breast, and said: "Wait, Ironheart, till I have spoken. Then! . . . . The words of Eagle Cry are true. He is great and wise, and has spoken all his heart. Red Fire is ready to be ruled by his chief, and to be his friend and speak for peace. But listen: If this shall be so, the girl Summer-Hair shall never marry a paleface. Her father shall swear by the sacred Sunstone that he will kill her first, even as our forefathers sacrificed the disobedient. . . . If this be so, then shall I be one with the Great Company and not hearken to the new Company, nor the voices of the Indians of the White Hand, but will fight the Great Company's battles, and in token will give my hand to Ironheart, if my brothers, whom I lead, are willing."

The young braves all made a motion of assent. Then Eagle Cry rose proudly, and said in a low stern tone—though in his heart he was dismayed—that he granted Red Fire's demand.

Then Red Fire stretched out his hand to the Factor, and they made their pact silently before the company. But neither loved the other, nor ever could. The reason why was clear to Red Fire, but not to Ironheart.

It was at this point that a messenger from the White Hands came from the old posthouse where they were quartered as guests, heavy with drink, and asking admittance. There were in all forty of the White Hands, led by a young chief called Breaking Tree. He was admitted, and Eagle Cry, rising, told him what the council had decided, and begged him to convey their greeting to the far tribes and the White Hands, but to say that they must remain friends with the Great Company. At this, Breaking Tree, who had heretofore been confident of the success of his mission, threw a malicious look at Ironheart, and cried out fiercely: "There is the white thief who steals away the minds of the Indians. He is of the big army of robbers. But we shall sweep

them away, as the grass before summer fire." Suddenly he raised his bow, with a fanatical whoop, at Ironheart. Some one seized his arm. The arrow sped, but, flying free of any in the council-room, it pierced the curtain behind which stood Summer-Hair. There was a cry. The curtain was swiftly drawn back, and disclosed the girl with an arrow quivering in her shoulder. A score of bows were drawn, but Eagle Cry, with his arm round his daughter, cried, "Let him go in peace; he is still our guest. There will come a time when the White Hands will lose a man for every drop of blood spilt here. But they shall go at once from our village, nor shall you give them food for their journey."

Breaking Tree left the tent, now thoroughly sobered. A hundred bows were drawn upon him and his followers, and with these menacing them, the White Hands left the village behind.

When they had gone another council was held, at which Ironheart spoke much; and the pipe of peace was smoked.

CHAPTER VIII.—A SIEGE AND PARLEY.

BRIAN KINGLEY had captured Fort Gabriel, making prisoners of two trappers who had been to it more caretakers than garrison. He expected that there would be fighting, but did not think that the Hudson's Bay Company would attempt a re-capture till the springtime. Fort Saviour, as he knew, was the nearest fort; but of the name of its chief factor he was ignorant. He did not, as we said elsewhere, relish fighting the followers of the Hudson's Bay Company, but he would not be the aggressor, and that would make the matter easier. Holding the fort against odds would be pleasant enough to him. He loved rather than avoided danger. Those were fighting days. Waterloo and Trafalgar were still news to the world and present topics to all British men; the Greeks were fighting for independence; war was in the air.

Brian had but thirty men—voyageurs, trappers, soldiers. He had but a small field of resources behind him, while the Hudson's Bay Company had resources practically unlimited, for they had a line of forts from which reinforcements could come. It was a forlorn hope; but the North West Company had promised him more men in the spring, and it was possible that the rising of the Indians might be successful, though this was not a matter which had his sympathy. Anything which roused the Indians against either company he considered an evil.

He set himself to work to put the fort in as good condition as was possible in winter. For a time he was busy enough. Then came days when there was nothing to do. He had little to read. He thought a good deal—more steadily than he had done for years. He occupied himself much with his past—not altogether pleasant in retrospect. With Scotland more than with Ireland. Was he becoming a renegade? When, once or twice, he thought of the flute which he heard distantly on the Red River—and he wished it were at Fort Gabriel, whoever played it—the songs he imagined lilting from it were not Irish but Scotch; not *Garry Owen and Glory*, but *The Bush aboon Traquair*. And when he thought of Scotland much, and of particular events of a certain year, he became disturbed, and longed for action to take the place of thoughts. This desire for activity at last overcame him. He had not the faculty for waiting possessed by Chief Factor Venlaw.

Two or three times a few men had been permitted to go out and look for moose, but they had been limited to certain boundaries, and had not been very successful. Brian, bored by his inactivity, determined at last to go out himself with a party. There seemed no pro   'ity of any attack from the Hudson's Ba   npany, and, in any case, those left be   . the fort would be able to resist an assault, and hold the place till the return of the sportsmen. There was the danger of being cut off from the fort, but that had to be risked.

One morning, very early, they issued forth. They would probably not have stepped so briskly, had they known that a band of the Hudson's Bay Company men were watching them from a pine grove not far from the fort. Brian had more than once debated on cutting down this grove, since it would afford a good cover for an attacking party, but he had hesitated because it sheltered the fort from the west winds. He contented himself with having it watched and regularly searched. He was not, however, aware that the grove contained a very effective hiding-place, which was likely to be known to the members of a Hudson's Bay Company party. This very morning, before the hunters started, there had been a search, but it was perfunctory, and the twenty odd men led by Chief Factor Venlaw lay concealed under the very noses of the searchers, who might easily have been captured had it been according to Venlaw's programme. He hoped, however, to employ strategy; the more so, because he

had heard one of the men from the fort speak of the projected hunt.

When the searchers returned to the fort, and soon afterwards he saw Brian and his handful of men issue forth, he determined on his plan of action. About noon would be the slackest time at the fort. Moreover, any one who might chance to pass out during the morning would be likely to return at noon. His action should be governed by this event, if it occurred. If not, another plan, based upon another supposition, should be put into play.

It was his intention to make a rush upon the gates at the moment any one should be entering, and so, if possible, enter the fort. A half-breed left the fort about nine o'clock, and they saw him returning about noon. The distance between the grove and the gates was about one hundred yards. Venlaw's men were all swift and noiseless runners, and were likely to accomplish the distance and do the thing successfully, though one would have said the odds were heavy against them.

The half-breed came slowly on, bearing a part of an animal he had killed on the shoulder between him and the grove, so that he could not, without removing it, or turning towards the pines, see any one in that direction.

Venlaw turned to his men. "Don't fire until I give the word; but enter the fort guns cocked, and cover every man that shows himself. Remember, capture, not bloodshed, is our aim. A pound of pemmican and three plugs of tobacco to each man, if we do the thing successfully. Keep close to me; speak no word. . . Are you ready?"

He raised his hand, holding it poised till the half-breed was almost at the gate, then he gave the signal, and with great swiftness they sped upon the fort. The half-breed did not hear them till the pad of moccasined feet was almost beside him, and at that moment the gate was opened. Before he could cry out a hand was clapped on his mouth, and he was drawn backwards to the ground, and Venlaw and his men rushed in before the gate could be closed upon them. The sentinel who had opened it, and another, stood an instant bewildered, then swung their guns shoulderwards, but Venlaw and one of his followers sprang upon them and seized the weapons. Both went off, but, fortunately, without injury to any one. The men were disarmed. The rest of the garrison now came armed and crowding through the doors of the fort to the yard. Venlaw's

" He sat down and dropped his forehead on his clenched fists."

followers instantly levelled their rifles at them.

The Factor raised his hand towards the besieged. "Don't fire, or attempt resistance," he said ; "it will be useless bloodshed. We are masters. The Hudson's Bay Company wishes only its rights. You have done your duty in obeying your captain, but now stack your arms, for I shall command you henceforth." The men were under cover of the rifles ; they saw that resistance must be made with great loss of life, and even then with little chance of success, and they dropped the butts of their guns upon the ground, still, however, holding them. One of the men— he who had been left in command—spoke. "What will you do with us, if we surrender ?"

"Take you over to Fort Saviour, and from there send you south of the Hudson's Bay country. Stack your arms !"

At that moment a woman who had accompanied the expedition appeared behind the men. She suddenly raised a pistol at the Factor, and fired. The bullet grazed his temple, bringing blood, and tore away a piece of his fur cap. He staunched the blood with his buck-skin glove, and it froze on his cheek as it came ; but for a moment he did not speak, and he did not change his position.

One of the men beside the woman seized her arm — it was her husband.

Venlaw spoke now, but not to his assailant. "Ground your arms," he said sternly to the group about the woman ; but she shrieked out,—" Fire on them ! fire on them ! O you cowards ; I could kill you myself !" She struggled in her husband's arms.

The captured men silently laid their rifles down ; and now the Factor spoke to the woman, his glove stiff with the blood from the still-bleeding wound. "You fight hardly fair ; and I'm not sure but what you gave you ought to get. You might have waited till you saw what we intended. You were foolish. But we will not quarrel with you, if you will get us a tin of tea and cook us some of this fresh meat,"—pointing to the venison which the disarmed and captured half-breed had brought,—"for we've had little enough to eat this two days past, and we have work to do yet to-day. And as for your husband, if he is here, I promise you shall go with him, wherever he goes."

The woman was overcome by the Factor's coolness and his quiet speaking. She stood for a moment as though dumbfounded, and then turned and went into the fort. Like most women of such impulses she was soon after as earnest in making the tea and cooking the venison as she had been in her murderous attack upon the Factor. Meantime, the prisoners were put in well-guarded rooms.

The weather grew colder as the day went on. Decisive preparations were made to receive Brian and his men. Towards sun-down a watchman gave the word that the hunters were returning. Venlaw formed his men advantageously, and more or less out of sight, in the yard, with instructions, as before, not to fire until he gave the word. Brian and his followers had had a successful day, and were in high spirits. On the fort the North West Company's flag was still flying. Venlaw was too cautious to think of lowering it yet. When within a few yards of the gates, one of Brian's half-breeds gave a sharp call as a signal for opening the gates. It was answered from within by one of the Factor's men. When the men were immediately at the gates they opened, and they came in eagerly, for they were hungry. Before they grasped the situation they were nearly all in, and then Brian became aware that rifles were threatening them from the windows of the fort, and from the yard. He saw that they were in a trap, but he was not inclined to yield tamely. He caught his rifle to his shoulder with his eye upon the leader of the invaders. On the instant he recognised this leader as Andrew Venlaw. He was dumbfounded. He lowered his gun. Behind him his followers were still crowding in at the gate, covered by the rifles.

The Factor stepped forward. "I think," he said, "it would be wiser to make no resistance. You have lost this game. Save your life for a better."

"Venlaw! Andrew Venlaw!" said the other, finding his voice.

"Yes, that is my name," was the cold reply. "Order your men to stack their arms. We have you at an advantage."

Brian glanced at the carcase of the moose which his men had brought with them, and with a little of his old humour answered: "We've got our venison at a price something unusual." Then he glanced round, saw the hopelessness of the position, and added: "Pile your arms, my men. We have lost Fort Gabriel."

His followers silently obeyed. Venlaw made a sign, and the prisoners were taken into the fort. Brian did not move, for the Factor motioned him to stay. When all were gone but they two, and a sentinel not within earshot, Venlaw spoke: "First, as to the matter of the fort. The North West Company surprised and stole this post. You were their chief robber."

Brian made a gesture of dissent, shrugged his shoulders, and said, with that old disdain remembered by Venlaw all too well,—"Indeed! You were always somewhat raw and unmannerly, Venlaw. Don't you think it were fairer to give a gentleman bite and sup, —from his own pillaged larder, after a long day's tramp—than to keep him freezing like this, with empty belly and choking throat, particularly when we bring fresh rations with us, bought, us I said, at war-famine prices. That done, I could easier grasp the fact of your presence in this wild land, and as my gaoler, Master Venlaw."

The Factor flushed to his hair. This Irishman had not changed since the days when he had mocked the young Scotsman on the fair-ground at Braithen. He answered, however, with some sarcasm in his tone, "I supposed that good soldiers and faithful officers thought of their duties first, and their bellies afterwards."

"Faith, then, Venlaw," retorted the other, "I see neither war nor duty here. Be-lad, you have us by the heels, and we must swing at your will. And what little there is to do officially in the way of surrender, can be performed, I think, in a warm room, and not in a freezing court-yard, and before a good dish of hot meat, and not on the flank of a cold carcase."

Venlaw was very angry, but his temper was well held behind his teeth. "You have a gay spirit," he replied; "we'll see if it holds good when time of reckoning comes. Meanwhile," waving his hand towards the door, at which a half-breed sentinel stood,

"An arrow quivering in her shoulder."

"this man will lead you where you'll find something to eat."

"Sure, then, my solemn and ubiquitous Scotsman," was the response, "I think I know the way; and when we meet at that hour of reckoning, I beg that you'll wear a face less like a hangman. 'Tis bad enough to be a prisoner, but to have a surly gaoler, who thinks he has the world's morals—and immorals—to guard, treble a man's punishment. Fellow-townsmen, like ourselves, shouldn't turn Gorgon when they meet in a foreign land. But! I remember, I gave you an invitation to meet me at the North Pole, or thereabouts. Well, here we are, and after supper . . . after supper . . . eh, Venlaw?" And Brian pushed on into the fort, where his face suddenly grew grave. He could have bitten his tongue out for that speech about their meeting again. The memory was a sad one to him now. But, as he said in his mind, "the fellow took himself so seriously and was so unbearably immaculate!"

Venlaw watched him disappear, then stood for a long time regardless of the still increasing cold, his closed fingers pressed to his mouth as though to hold the words bursting from his lips. He was thinking—thinking, with the result of ten years' waiting in his grasp. The man was in his power that had made him an exile from his country, robbed him of love and home, and spoiled the life of her who was the angel of his boyhood, the hope of his young manhood. "It shall be done," he said, and dropped his hand upon his leg with a thud. And Chief Factor Venlaw had a fashion of keeping his word.

A couple of hours later, Venlaw sent for Brian. When the latter entered, and the door closed behind him, the two were face to face, alone.

"Well, Chief Factor Venlaw," said Brian, with an assumed yet effective nonchalance, "what function do you purpose now?"

"Only one," was the business-like reply. "First, I may tell you that your men will be taken to Fort Saviour." He paused.

"And for myself?"

"And for yourself—hereafter." The Factor's voice was still quiet, yet stern. Then he continued: "And now, Brian Kingley, we have some things to settle."

"More things to settle?" rejoined Brian, lifting his eyebrows ironically. "What are they?"

"Have you forgotten the last time we met? or do—gentlemen—like you, remember nothing that they care to forget?"

A tone of seriousness now came into Brian's voice. "Venlaw," he said, "you mean that day at Beltane Fair, when I swung a lass out of your arms, and took a kiss for a slight debt she owed me. Faith, it was pretty but insolent play. I'll admit, Venlaw, that I'm sorry for it now." Brian meant infinitely more apology than he expressed; and he would have expressed it all, but he found it hard to do it in the circumstances, with this man sitting as a judge over him.

"What you did to me was nothing; but you spoiled a girl's life. You spoiled Jean Fordie's life."

Brian flushed suddenly, and his words came sharp and hot. "Venlaw, you lie!"

Venlaw got threateningly to his feet, and his eye ran sharply to the other's. "You shamed and ruined the sister of your friend."

"Again, Venlaw, you lie!" Brian's voice was harsh, and his hands clenched on the table before him, as he looked up.

The Factor's face had now an iron-like hardness. He had resolved upon one way, and he would not be changed from it.

"It was her brother's or her father's place to bring you to punishment," he persisted, "else I had done it before I left Braithen. You ran away from the father, and helping the brother—for your own safety, maybe—kept the truth from him all these years. Now, I have to do the brother's will. I gladly do it. If he could have met you here he would have killed you. But he could not. He charged me to do it, for her wrongs, his, and my own; and, by Heaven, I will!"

Brian, amazed, had risen to his feet slowly. He said in a low tone, his voice roughened with bitterness,—"It is all false, Venlaw; false, as I'm a man! I did not ruin her.'

"But you are no man; you are a poltroon, a coward!" The words came with very scorn.

Brian stepped forward, his face full of fury and his body shaking. "I'll trench that lie in your blood, my low-born Scotsman, if you dare meet me, tossing sword-points."

"You shall not lack for opportunity," was the quick reply. "And to encourage you, I would remind you that I have been waiting ten years to have my hour out with you."

"You always were a talker, Venlaw."

"And you a drunken idler, there and here."

"Faith, I'll not plead innocence of that, before so perfect a judge. I see you have been reading the records of the Hudson's Bay Company. You ever had a taste for scandal," was the reply, with malicious sarcasm.

" You have lost this game."

"I read no records. I have been here ten years. I saw them acted — saw you act them."

"Well, we've a pretty account to square, and I'll thank you if you'll talk less and do more."

"We cannot fight here," said Venlaw; "not within the fort. But the plains are wide, and the moon is bright."

Brian had now recovered his coolness; he even spoke with a grim and deadly humour. "When you will. Why not at the moose-yard, a mile or so away to the south?—A noble cock-pit, where we may have our game on a smooth and solid table."

Venlaw thought a minute, looking harshly at the other, and then said: "Yes, I know the place. But one of us must fall, and how shall the other be cared for?"

"Calculating ever, shepherd, but not inventive. Why, if I fall, you can send your men to bury me, or carry me, where they will. If you fall—well, you'd better provide for that by leaving word here where they may find you. Be precise in that, Chief Factor, for I have a presentiment that you shall come back in carriage horizontal—while I must take the plains again, or have

a wild minute with your rascally comrades here, to be eaten without salt, if I hear they stand well by you; as is likely, for you and they are savages, my hillsman.

Venlaw was quite cool, his face inscrutable; his eyes had a resolute shadow and a directness almost oppressive to a lesser man than Brian. But the North had given them both of its intrepidity, and neither blenched before the other. Brian's was a fine face, the more pleasant of the two, as his form was the more graceful and closely knit. He stood with a hand on his hip, and his other arm resting on a high desk near, at ease, yet alert and forceful. The other looked honest, strenuous, impregnable—a leader of men.

A sudden silence came between them. The candle flickered, and the eyes of both fell on it mechanically, stayed a moment, then met. They were both, that instant, thinking of Beltane Fair; Venlaw revengefully, bitterly; the other remorsefully, for the event was doubling on him thoroughly. He loved the woman now in memory as in present fact, and through his fault she had evidently been slandered. Venlaw believed her guilty. Well, he should pay for that. If he himself fell, he should only be getting his due. And so, now for the end of it!

Venlaw spoke. "I will leave word as you say; also, that in case I am killed you are not to be followed. And now, what shall it be—swords or pistols?"

"For old acquaintance' sake, swords! I see you wear one, and mine is in the fort. I should like to prove, after all these years, that I'm still your master in war, as I did once when we were youths; and in love—as I also did once before." Immediately these words were uttered Brian regretted them, for he did not mean them; but he could not help torturing this man.

The hands of the other trembled slightly as they rested on the table, but he spoke no word directly. He tapped upon the door with the sheath of his sword. One of his men entered.

"Confine the prisoners for the night," he said; "then bring me the keys of the gates and the doors. There is no necessity for a watch. Mr. Kingley will remain in this room. You will bring buffalo skins here for a bed, and some food."

Then the two men were left alone again.

"At midnight I will come again," said Venlaw, with his hand on the door. "We will go then."

"At twelve, as you say, shepherd,—and you shall travel far!" and, turning his back, Brian sought the fire. The door opened and Venlaw went out.

CHAPTER IX.—THAT INFINITE EDGE.

THERE was no wind in the woods, and if you had listened you would have heard only the sighing of cedars weighted by the snow, or the occasional crack of a burdened limb. You might even have caught the long breath of a sleeping moose, but little more. You would have found it very cold too if you were not used to cold. But just when the world seemed all a frosty dream, a beautiful solitary mummy, which might wake again after thousands of years, and one would have been tempted to join in the white wonder of that repose, a faint, delightful sound came floating out of the night. It was a low, clear note, impelled by some Orpheus of the frozen North, like the exquisite contralto whistle of an organ, muffled in a weft of filmy cloud, as though the trees were breathing the song through their frost.

It grew and grew, scarcely becoming louder, but more distinct, more sweet and piercing. It came very near, and was accompanied now by the soft patter of feet. These were strange things. It was as if some minstrel of the dead was sauntering with his companions through those ancient fastnesses.

Presently, an Indian girl and an old man appeared. The girl's lips might have sent forth this music, so warm and eloquent were they—a protest against this smileless world about them, eyed distantly by the presiding moon. There was with her an old man wintered with age, but pervading this snowy arena with that strange music, which, but a moment before, seemed almost supernatural. His instrument was a flute. Soon he took it from his lips, and spoke. "It's bitter cold for this, but I said before I left the old land that when I got within sight of the place where he was I'd play one of the tunes they crooned over him when a child, and I've done it—fantastic enough, maybe, and with a frozen finger." He could hardly have played thus on the open plains. In the woods it was not so cold.

"You are a strange man," said the girl, and she caught the white and clammy finger and rubbed it well with snow. Then the old man clothed his hands, and they ran on together.

"You are nearly as much an angel as he is a man," said the old man to the girl, "for I should never have reached him were it not for you. You are wonderful."

"The ways of the Spirits are wonderful," she replied musingly and a little sadly, "and cruel too—— See, there, again, is the fort. Our journey will soon be over."

"But look!—look there! What is that?" cried the old man suddenly.

And what they saw is now to be told.

When, at midnight, Andrew Venlaw and Brian Kingley stepped out from the fort, there was a marvellous silence on the plains. In the woods slight sounds could be heard, but on the plains nothing was alive; nothing, indeed, in the world seemed alive, except the stars and the moon, prying, speculative, uncompanionable.

They walked side by side. Brian turned round once or twice to look at the fort. Again once or twice he scanned the plains. He was impressed by the austerity of the earth, the cold imperturbable sky. Death were better here than in more friendly places; the world were not so hard to leave. He was interested in the thing itself — its strangeness, its savage contradictions. He cast an inquiring glance at the face of the man beside him. It was, such of it as could be seen, most serious and absorbed. The man appeared unconscious of his companion's presence. Something in his look brought a flash of grave drollery to the other's eyes. Surely the owner of those eyes must jest, if even grimly, upon this man to the end!

Their steps fell evenly, but made, with their moccasined feet, only the softest sound on the snow. Their arms almost touched as they walked. With that droll look playing on his face, Brian presently began to hum, with a half-tender, half-mocking cadence, the words of an old song:—

" And when will you be coming back, my bold cavalier,
With the gold upon your shoulder, and my ribbon on your breast?
For I know a gallant waiting, and they whisper in my ear,
That, of true loves and new loves, the last love is best."

At that they came to the edge of the moose-yard, and both stepped into it; it was slightly lower than the plain, tramped smooth by the hoofs of the moose. Brian repeated the last two lines of the verse. Venlaw's teeth clinched. Perhaps, unintentionally, Brian forgot to mock, and threw some quaint reflected feeling into them, an airy pathos, which struck into Venlaw's heart suddenly and surprisingly. He fastened his eyes on Brian's face. Unaccountably, then, there came to him a sense of that ineffaceable comradeship of race; perhaps something more. He felt what he had never before done to this man—a strange and deep sympathy. The solemnity of the occasion moved him. Might there have been some mistake after all?

Brian was whipping his sword lightly on the icy air, as if to get its balance.

"Now," Venlaw said, with a burst of blundering frankness, "own that you did wickedly. For it's an ill thing to go to your Maker with a falsehood on your lips, Brian Kingley."

Any other kind of speech might have influenced Brian. This could only rouse resentment in him. The Factor's tactlessness, the recapture of the fort, the humiliation he had thereby suffered, and, more than all, the false accusation against Jean,—for he was now as much her champion as Venlaw—sent a sharp reply to his lips.

"I knew you were a bit of a braggart, shepherd, but I did not guess that you'd tremble at honest fighting with a sword in your hand. I said you lied, and you did; and I'm ready to trench the lie in your blood, as I said. So here's salutation to you, Venlaw,——and good-bye to you!"

They saluted, then stood to position. At that instant a faint, delicate sound came over the snow to them distantly. They

looked round. The plains were silent, save for this. Far to the north these everlasting hummocks of white, reaching to the Pole; the granite integrity of frost absorbing them; the multitudinous circles of icy years around them.

They drew back from each other. Their faces became very pale, for the music came penetratingly, sweetly to them. And it was a melody to which one had been cradled, and the other knew in pleasant, familiar hills; it was, indeed, sometimes sung to the very verses that but now fell from Brian's lips. They stood not moving, their swords drawn, the points poised, the blades flashing in the moonlight. They seemed to listen for years. Suddenly with a swift impulse the music faded, and was gone.

And astonished beyond words,—though they both thought the thing a trick of the imagination,—but determined still, the two men faced each other. Still their swords hung inactive. The respite seemed a mutual wish. They scarcely moved for a few minutes. Presently Brian raised his sword. His opponent's lifted also. The points caught and wrangled. They sawed and clashed, played angrily, drew back for a last precipitation of energy, and caught again wickedly. Suddenly there was a sound as of hurrying feet, then a call, and the approach of two figures. But they did not stop. Immediately a girl jumped down into the yard and ran against the swords, throwing them up.

"Ironheart! Ironheart!" she cried.

It was Summer-Hair.

Then a man caught the Factor's arm. "Andrew Venlaw!" said a voice dissuasive and reproachful.

Venlaw dazedly turned upon him and said hoarsely, "Benoni!"

"So, I've just come in time," rejoined Benoni, wheeling now towards Brian. "Of all the years that have gone since you left the old land, and of all the days, 'tis strange that you should fly at each other's throat the moment I bear down upon you."

Brian looked hard at him, then drew his hand swiftly across his eyes.

"Before God, 'tis strange enough!" he said.

"And why should you fight?" continued the old man. "Aren't there Indians and other wild beasts to be killed without riddling the world of a white man where white men are few, and no need for your swords going rusty? Clank them back into their scabbards, for I've a word to say to you both that'll flush your faces with shame for many a day, however cold the wind blows.".

The two men dropped their swords into the sheaths, not yet speaking. Summer-Hair stood a little apart, looking at the Factor inquiringly, anxiously. At last Venlaw said: "You've come—from home, Benoni. Why?"

The reply was impressive. "There were two men, brave men! and they went mad one day. For, one did a light thing to a girl in the face of the world, and the other did a wrong thing when he would not trust the girl. Ill was spoken of her. The years went on, and the two who should have been there to set her right before the world, were waiting a chance, in another land, to bury their swords in each other—— But 'tis cold here for those that are not fighting, and if we may go on to the fort our story can be finished there."

The Factor nodded, and now, silent, they walked back to the fort abreast, the girl beside Benoni. Once the Factor turned, and, as if it had just occurred to him, held out his hand to Summer-Hair. "You showed Benoni the way, Summer-Hair?" he asked.

The girl nodded, but she did not speak. Again there was silence. Presently Brian said: "Benoni, were you playing on your flute just before you came?"

"As good a tune as ever was played out of heaven."

"Well," rejoined Brian, with a laugh which was half a sigh, "it blocked the way to heaven to one of us. For had you not played as you did, and detained the wrangle of our swords for a minute, you had come upon a dead man in the moose-yard."

"I don't know which one was to be the murderer," said Benoni, "but I do know that both of you are well this side of heaven till you've cleared the name of an innocent girl."

They spoke no more until they came to the fort. The gates creaked slowly outwards, and Venlaw was the last to enter. Before he did so he turned round and faced the empty plains. A desert of sand is sad and terrible in its desolation, but there is something majestic in a desert of snow, even when it strikes with millions of deadly needles through the heart. For, at its worst it has no torture, only God-like sleep. The Factor, looking back, thought soberly, not weakly, of how a waiting grave had been foiled of an occupant. At that moment there was in him the spirit of the North, which makes men brave, if it does not render them merciful. He thought of a day, ten years before, when he bade good-bye to Scotland. He paused

longer than he knew. A hand touched him on the arm.

"Ironheart," Summer-Hair's voice said, "when one comes to my father's lodge my father does not stand in the doorway, but hurries to give him welcome."

"I am forgetful," he replied, and he looked kindly at the girl. They entered the fort. The Factor roused some of his men, and a meal was prepared. When it was over Summer-Hair was led to another room, where she might sleep. The three men remained where they were. For a time nothing was said. Then Venlaw briefly explained to Benoni the occurrence of the day before, and the position of Brian and his followers. When that was done Benoni began to speak. Quietly he drew the picture of Jean's early life, of her mother's death, her love for her brother, and her devotion to her father—of her as she was in the old Castle, at her household duties, or at the loom; as she appeared in the streets, modest, admired, discreet; as in the church, reverent; as in the dance, blithe yet reserved; as always good and true.

Then, while they sat subdued, wondering at the simple power of the old man's recital, all Brian's assumed irony and nonchalance gone, all Venlaw's sombreness modified, Benoni spoke gravely of Bruce's crime, and of the anxious days preceding Beltane Fair; of the occurrence at the fair itself, briefly, firmly, severely.

"A man's only a man," he said, "and I've seen the day when the brush of a lip was pleasant enough to me. But the deed done that day was more than an idle thing." Here his voice became low, as if to speak was a trouble.

"You, Andrew Venlaw, listened to a woman who sought to make bad blood between you and Jean Fordie, and you believed the woman you loved—the plaything of this man."

Then he told them of Elsie's confession.

During his last words strange changes passed over the faces of the listeners; both became pale, and Venlaw rose from his seat. "Is this so?" he said, with a despairing voice.

"It is true," replied Benoni, and he drew from his breast a letter from Elsie, and bade Venlaw read it. The Factor took it, his hand trembling. When he had finished Brian took it from his fingers. Venlaw dropped into a seat, unhappy and dismayed. When Brian had finished reading he leaned his elbow on the table and covered his face.

"She has endured this shame ten years,"

said Benoni. He paused. Still neither man spoke.

"There have been two cowards in the world for ten years and more," he continued. Venlaw and Brian caught each other's eyes, and sprang to their feet.

"What can we do?" questioned Venlaw manfully.

"Is there any way?" hoarsely added Brian. "Before God," he added more loudly, "I'd buy back these ten years with my life if I could. Listen to me, Venlaw. For the thing done that morning I've had shame enough ever since, and I'd not cry quits to whatever punishment might come.—— But what's to be done now? There's the trouble."

Benoni came forward so that he had the two men, one on either side of him, and said: "There is this to be done, that you shake hands like men and forget your quarrel, and when that's over I have more to say." He put a hand on the shoulder of both.

Silently the two men clasped hands.

"Now," continued the showman, "there's this further to do; for it's what I've come for, and what I'll not go back without: from Braithen you came, leaving trouble behind you; to Braithen you must go back to right that trouble so far as you can. I've travelled the seas and these wild lands for this, old man as I am."

"And what can I do by going back," said Brian, "since Elsie knows the truth and Bruce knows it, and she has spoken, and Bruce and I can do the same from here?" And here he sighed, and a bitter smile passed across his face. He felt that if any went back to Jean, naturally it should be Andrew. He was sure the old man meant that, and, of course, Jean also. And so he said: "For the rest 'tis Venlaw should go back. 'Tis he that's needed when all's righted."

Benoni now saw how Brian was being punished. He had probed the heart of the man's secret. He was glad, and yet sorry too.

Here the Factor, who had stood muffling his beard at his mouth as though to blockade emotion, spoke slowly: "If there is any to stay it must be I. But, as I take it, we both should go. For I long to see the old land once again, and there is the grave of my old friend the Dominie I'd visit, and justice to be done altogether!"

Benoni's face lighted up. He tapped them both on the arms decisively. "You will both come," he said. "For the last words she spoke to me when I stood on the Castle steps at parting were these: 'If one comes both should, for both did wrong, and forgiveness does not carry easily across the sea.'—— So, will you come, or will you stay? —both come or both stay, it must be."

"It is not easy on the instant to say that it shall be done, and yet it shall," responded Andrew.

"I am a prisoner," rejoined Brian, "and, faith! I've duty to do here, as well as Venlaw, when the chance comes again; but I'll go—and gladly—at the hour you say, if I can; and there's my word on it!"

Once again Benoni spoke. "The lass will break her heart if Bruce does not come back with you, but I fear it is not safe. For though he mightn't lose his life, he'd forfeit his freedom. But I'd give much to see the lad,—I call you all lads yet, though you are men in the full wash of years—and carry a message from him to her."

The Factor assured him that he should meet Bruce soon, and told him of the expedition against the White Hands, and of the movement he was soon to make towards Fort Mary.

The candle spluttered and went out, and only the light of the fire played upon the faces of the men. They drew about it, and smoked a pipe of peace. And the hours wheeled on, and when sleep found them Brian and Venlaw lay together under the same blankets.

While these things were happening two women sat beside a fire in Braithen, and there was bundled up on the floor beside them an idiot, who muttered to himself and blew bubbles from a basin at his side.

"Elsie," said one, "I shall always think that the poor lad here has done more for us than we for ourselves, for he it was that made us friends and killed the wrong between us, and sent Benoni across the seas." She paused.

"And sent Benoni across the seas to bring Andrew back to you," shyly said the other.

"To bring Andrew and Brian back," gravely added Jean.

And the idiot, as the fleecy spheres of water lifted away towards the ceiling, or fled shuddering into the flame of the chimney, muttered,—"Oh, eh, pretty bird, come back soon—— Oh, oh, the white horses—— Ride away—— Oh, pretty Else!"

CHAPTER X.—THE BLOW AND THE REBOUND.

A WEEK later found Chief Factor Venlaw and his prisoners at Fort Saviour. A stout band of men had been left to garrison Fort

Gabriel, and these were speedily reinforced by Indians from Eagle Cry's tribe. Venlaw was determined that the redeemed post should not again pass out of the hands of the Hudson's Bay Company. There was little to fear that any immediate demonstration would or could be made by the North West Company, for the news of this defeat would take long to travel to headquarters. A surprise could not easily be effected again.

Never in the course of its history had the Hudson's Bay Company been threatened as it was at present. If they were defeated, it would tell hard against the white man in the country. The North West Company had not played a noble game. As much from vanity and jealousy as anything else it encroached upon these areas where the Hudson's Bay Company had honourably and firmly made its position. Under the name of protest against a great monopoly, it actually shook the general friendship of the Indians for the white man. The White Hands, if they succeeded, intended, despite their protestations of friendship for the North West Company, to begin a war of race.

At Fort Saviour, Venlaw strengthened his position, gathered friendly bands of Indians to unite with the Sun Rocks, and sent *coureurs-des-bois* to other forts south, suggesting plans of resistance and schemes of action if they should be necessary. Since that notable day when Summer-Hair was wounded, her tribe had been enthusiastically staunch and undivided in their loyalty to Ironheart and the Great Company. Red Fire kept bravely to his compact with the Factor and Eagle Cry. But the old chief was not so certain that the result of that compact would be well for him in the end. He knew now that Summer-Hair loved Venlaw, and he himself had not been indisposed to seal his friendship with the Hudson's Bay Company by giving his daughter in marriage to the Factor. But these are matters above the will of red man or of white. You shall more easily bind the wind than a man's or maid's desire, and nothing befalls as we ordain : not more now than when Euripedes told tales of his old Greeks and their loves and slaughters. And it will be so until there be no more love or slaughter.

The Factor's task was a huge one. With Eagle Cry and his Indians they must coincide with the forces from Fort Mary, attacking the White Hands from both sides. The village of the White Hands was in the Long Valley beyond the Big Sleep Woods. Venlaw's policy was, in this case, to assume the aggressive. The White Hands were not likely to make a move until spring. He would, therefore, march upon them at once and strike a decisive blow before the hostile forces could begin their horrible policy of waylaying and massacring stray travellers, or should seriously disturb the trade of the year. They would strike through to the west, relieving and reinforcing each garrison as they went. The Company must now maintain its position with a power and sharp demonstration, or subject itself in the future to constant attack and harassment.

Not the least anxious for the expedition to start was Benoni. He looked forward to meeting Bruce. That done, his embassy was over and he would return. He and Summer-Hair were the staunchest of friends. She questioned him unwearyingly concerning the world in which Jean Fordie played a part so important to the lives of several people. When he first came to the fort, asking for Chief Factor Venlaw, she had vaguely suspected (what woman does not suspect every possible thing as bearing on her happiness when she loves?) that this man's arrival would affect her. She had never rested till she had got at some clue to the truth. Then, as might not have been expected in a " savage," she offered to lead Benoni herself to Fort Gabriel. Her father objected, but, because he saw she was determined, sent an Indian with her and Benoni. The rest of the tribe did not know where she had gone. The Indian had become ill by the way and had to return, so she went on alone with the showman.

Benoni had read her secret. He thought nothing for her could come of it, and so at last to turn her thoughts away from Venlaw he told her of Jean, and of Andrew's love for her, in as careful and delicate a fashion as he could. Meanwhile he became popular with the Indians, for, with his flute, he took their barbarous airs and gave them melody and fancy, and filled their lodges with a new wild music. He had caught the spirit of the North, this amazing old Mercury.

Arrayed in flaring feathers of war, with their painted faces and garnished buckskins, they listened to him, in a great group, the night before they marched. The trees were just beginning to send forth their timid and juicy leaves. The snow had melted and slackened away along the wide sluices of the plains, the birds came sojourning from the south, and the grass rose cleansed and eager like velvet to feel for the foot of man. The air and earth exuded freshness; through the pores of the trees came the sweet sweat of their

"They sawed and clashed."

sap; from the bandages of that mummy Winter the jocund Spring stepped forth incarnated, encouraging. And in the heart of this Spring, through long flumes of its young breath, Benoni sent his flotilla of melodies.

He tossed the blood in the veins of the red men with the exhilarating music of battle, spun down the drives of time from barbarous minstrels of the hills; he charged their bodies with the miraculous pulse of his own temperament—a punchinello, a common showman, an artist!

Then he suddenly detached himself from these clarion chords, and, casting his eyes on Venlaw and Brian, played with great softness melodies familiar to them both. They were going out to battle; and, in any case, it was best that they should be steeped in memories and go forth like gentlemen wearing the favours of their ladies on their arms. For such live better and die better, and fight ere they die with more valiant arm.

In the morning they tried to dissuade Benoni from going, for, as they said, he was old, and the march would be severe. But he laughed at them, and said that he had marched many a mile with better men, and fought with as good, by sea and land. That his hair was grey was nothing. The hunger of travel was on him, and he had a lad to meet beyond. Besides, two of his friends were going, and there was an end of it!

Yes, *they* were going, for Brian had said, because they were going back to Scotland together if they returned from this enterprise, and because these Indians were the enemies of all white men, he would fight with and for the Hudson's Bay Company in this case if he were given permission. His duty had only been with Fort Gabriel, not with the intrigues of his masters with the Indians. This Andrew gladly gave.

For many days they travelled without sign of any foe. They reinforced two forts and two posts, and at last came to the Big Sleep Woods, beyond which were Long Valley and the village of the White Hands. A scout had brought them word that the White Hands had had the dance of the Black Knife,—the prelude to war,—and were just ready to march. He said that they had formed themselves into two groups, one evidently intended to march west on Fort Gabriel, and the other east towards Fort Saviour. Venlaw decided to attack at once.

He pushed forward, but suddenly found himself attacked. His men fought splendidly, and drove the Indians slowly back upon their village. Here a sharp struggle took place. It was a straining tangle of battle. Presently the White Hands were reinforced by a band which came hurrying down on the village from the north. It is hard to tell how the battle would have gone had help not come also to Venlaw. He had calculated his chances well. His plan of campaign had succeeded. For, in the nick of time, there came speeding from the west the forces from Fort Gabriel, under command of Bruce Fordie. The junction had been providentially achieved. The enemy gave way, and were forced to retreat. After the moment of the turn of battle Bruce came face to face with Brian. Venlaw had not counted upon this. He had not foreseen that a collision might occur. In Bruce's veins the fret of anger and battle ran high. He drew a pistol instantly upon Brian.

"You here, you coward! I gave the thing to Venlaw to do. He has failed me. I do my own work now. Fight! Fight! or, by Heaven, I will kill you."

Brian stretched out his hand swiftly. "Don't fire, Bruce; don't fire! Listen to me!"

But at that instant a bullet from Bruce's pistol caught Brian in the shoulder, and he staggered back. Venlaw had seen the two meet and had rushed forward, but somewhat too late, though he caught Brian as he fell. Bruce stood with smoking pistol, the weft of battle loosening from about them. He was dazed and uncertain.

"No more of that, Bruce," said the Factor. "You and I have been playing a mad game, for the man is innocent of the worst."

"Innocent! Innocent! You swore him guilty two months ago."

"No matter. I speak truth now. Here, bear a hand. Cut down this coat to see what hurt you've done him."

Brian had fainted. When he became conscious he found Bruce and Benoni beside him. He smiled up into Bruce's face. "Faith, you greet an old comrade rarely, Master Bruce," he said. "The bite of your kiss is a wild one." Then a grave look came into his eyes. "But, maybe, it'll help a little to make even the debt I owe you and yours."

For reply Bruce pressed his old friend's hand: but said (he knew all now), "You did wrong, Brian, but I believe you meant no evil, and I'm sorry I've hurt you."

Brian shook his head. "Bedad, no! I meant no harm, but harm has come, and I'm getting a little of what I deserve. And there's the truth!"

The showman's not unskilful surgery extracted the bullet, and he gave it as his opinion that Brian would suffer no permanent injury, but would, on the contrary, be himself again in a few weeks.

On this side of the Atlantic they had now settled all accounts.

The White Hands were completely routed. Their chief was brought in a prisoner. And so ended the most notable struggle of the Indians of the North against the peaceful conquests of the Hudson's Bay Company; for the pride of the hostile Indians was broken; they were subdued; they sought peace, and kept it, much to the confusion of the rival company. And from Fort Jacques in the far west to Fort Saviour in the east, and straight across the wild wastes of Labrador to the cold wash of the sea, the great Company of Adventurers resumed their strong sovereignty.

CHAPTER XI.—THE TENT CURTAIN OUTWARD SWINGS.

THE return to Fort Saviour was accomplished successfully for Brian, and without new dangers for the expedition. A few score of braves and a handful of half-breeds never returned; but for those who part this world in righteous battle there is honest and righteous slumber, and sods lie lightly on them. There was mourning in the lodges of the Sun Rocks, but there was rejoicing too; for happiest they of all the world who welcome back the warrior from the well-fought field. The wives and maids were dressed in soft garnished buckskin, and moccasins of their most industrious and artistic hours. Among these Summer-Hair was first and last. Red Fire had got himself renown at Long Valley—he had the gift of bravery. But though he strutted through the camp in his comeliness and valour it had no charm for her. Yet Red Fire waited; for he had heard, as had all, that the Chief Factor was going back to the land of the palefaces; and he was a wise fellow among a foolish people. He conceived that the present lover with present gifts achieves most with woman. But Summer-Hair was silent. She was not as other women; there was in her veins some strain of ancient pride and sensitiveness. She knew of that fair woman over seas, yet she had taken Benoni to Venlaw, believing, at the same time, that this was death to her own hopes. She grew grave and graver; almost her only companions were Benoni and the wild deer she had tamed. It is possible that in their ears she had poured out her mind; but then, dumb creatures are like Heaven itself—they take all confidence, they give all sympathy, but they are silent, faithful.

Weeks, months, passed; Brian's wound had healed. He had been released, and had

THE CHIEF FACTOR

West Company to go upon that journey back
to Scotland, or to resign his commission if
need be;—and the need was very probable
after the part he had taken against the White
Hands. He was to sail from Montreal and
meet the others in London.

In the middle of summer the time came
for Andrew and Benoni to go. A chief trader
had come to take the Factor's place during
his absence, though it was possible, as Benoni
thought, that he might never return. His
little company of *voyageurs* were ready for
the start. The eve of his departure had
arrived. He had now come face to face with
his past and his future; he stood upon the
bridge between. All the struggles, the fighting, the endurance, the manly hardships, and
the conquests of the last ten years were about
him. The Indians that he had subdued were
his friends; the men to whom he had been a
stern but just master were his firm adherents.
He had no comrades; but men of his faculty
and power seldom have. Masterful minds
are solitary.

He sat in his office alone. The last stroke
of the pen had been given, the last necessary
command; his office had been handed over
to another.

It was nightfall; in the morning he should
go. Every item of life about him became
distinct. A blue-bird was whistling its last
notes in the trees without; he heard with
interested complacency the tramp of the
tame bear in the yard of the fort, its chain
rattling after it. His watch ticked on the
nail where it had hung, winter and summer, since he had come to Fort Saviour; he
looked at it now mechanically, yet fascinated
by it; its keen, strong pulsations were suited
to the time, for his brain was sensitively
active, and his heart was beating almost
painfully. These new sensations were strange
to him; he could not define them. To a man
better versed in the language of impressions
it would have been known as undefined
regret. Regret for what? Even that he
could not tell. He was going to see again
the woman he had loved since he was a little
child, whatever it might bring to him. He
was leaving—what? Here his thoughts
numbed; he forgot the world, himself. The
watch ticked on, and through the ticking, as
though it came from a great distance, he
heard presently the word, "Ironheart!"

He did not stir. Then a hand touched his
shoulder. "Ironheart," said the voice again.
He looked up. Summer-Hair stood beside
him.

"I am come to say good-bye," she said, as
his eyes turned to hers.

"I was coming to see you in the morning
before I started, Summer-Hair," he replied.
"I went to your father's lodge, but I could
not find you."

"I am here," she rejoined simply. "I have
brought you these, for the white chieftainess
over the seas. She drew forth a beautiful
wampum belt, hung with virgin gold and
bright metal, and a pair of moccasins deftly
and gloriously embroidered. "The belt is for
her waist, as the great girdle of white in the
sky; and the moccasins are for her feet, as
for those who walk the stars. The Indian
girl sends messages to her who loves Ironheart."

Venlaw took the gifts and gently said:
"Summer-Hair, I will take the gifts, for the
white chieftainess will love them; but you
are wrong—she has not given her love to
me."

The girl drew back. "You are a great
man," she said, with an inflection of doubt,
as though there was no woman but must love
him; "besides, she sent for you."

He smiled, and shook his head sadly.
"That is another thing."

"You will come back?" said the girl.

"I do not know," was his reply. "My
arm works best here, my life fits in."

"The deer are wonderful upon the plains,
the flesh of the moose is sweet; and the
lodges of the red men are warm with welcome. You *will* come back," she urged. "I
have read the sun upon the Sunstone on
Waiting Hill, and it says so."

She smiled. He was in a reverie. He
turned to the window facing the south.
The moon stole in on a broad ribbon of light.
The watch ticked loudly. Presently he
roused himself, and looked round to speak.
But the girl was gone; and he did not see
her again before he left.

The next dawn, however, when he and his
half-breeds stole away gaily towards the
south, a figure stood beside the Sunstone
on Waiting Hill, and watched them. Once
he looked back, but he did not see her;
and she remained there until they were
specks upon the horizon, and were swal-
lowed in the light of day. Then she sat
down by the stone and watched the sun beat
on it.

She sat till noon, not moving, but watching. Then she rose and said, retreating
backwards from it,—"Nothing speaks since
he has gone; the signs have gone with
him."

CHAPTER XII.—"THO' 'TWERE TEN THOUSAND MILE."

It is an autumn day in Braithen. The Shiel, fed by the early rains, grows to its banks, and here and there overflows. The hill-sides are still purple with heather, and the woods about Cowrie Castle are a grand mosaic of colour. The yews, the pines, the rowans, and the oaks, are harmonious in the modulations of colour. Jean Fordie has come to the top of the tower, her habit of an evening, to see the sun ride out beyond the hills, and to take a good-night look at the town, whose buildings ambled beside the river in easy irregularity. Perhaps, to herself, she had never absolutely admitted that each morning and evening she looked towards the south, along that steep road belting the hills, if haply she might see someone travelling towards the town—some old friends from another land. If hope deferred makes the heart sick, expectancy makes the face young; and from the first she never doubted —such was the buoyancy of her nature— that these old friends would return. What should happen when they did come was not so clear. But she saw justice ahead; and justice, to her, was now greater than love. For she had suffered an injustice, and she knew that it was crueller than unsatisfied affection.

She leaned against the bartisan wall, her eyes upon the south, thinking; and only seeing the horizon lying dimly beyond. Presently, she raised her head with a quick gesture of interest. There were three horsemen on the crest of the hill. Of course, she could not see who they were, but there came to her a swift instinctive conviction. The colour heightened in her cheek, and warmed her eye, and sent her fingers trembling to her hair. She watched them until they disappeared into a glen; and then she went below. It was natural, perhaps, that while she waited for something, she dared not think what, she should turn to the loom, where so many waiting hours had been passed.

Her hand was steady; the shuttle shot back and forth with clacking music, and once or twice she paused to move her hand gently across the cloth. But, from the smile upon her face, one would have said it was a distant, not a near, thing, which occupied her mind.

There came a gentle knocking at the door of the room. She started up, moved forward a little, and then paused. "Come in," she said.

Elsie Garvan entered. "Ye look sae strange," said Elsie;—"by a' the warl' gin I were a ghost; as surely ye wer'na lookin' for me."

Jean laughed a little nervously and said: "I dinna ken what I expected, Elsie: but, come here," she added, "for I hae a thing to say." Her eyes were bright.

"Is it that the waitin's ower?" said the other; "is it that they've come?"

"I am no sure," answered Jean, "but I hae a feeling."

Then in a low voice they talked together. . . . And three horsemen turned upon the town, not far away, and talked together also. These paused at the top of a brae, and looked down into the valley where the town reposed. And one said: "Faith, I'm thinking, 'twas but yesterday I roared for another pot of beer at the Rob Roy, and not ten years ago."

"Many a man's gone for ever from Braithen town since then," rejoined a little man at his left.

"There's Cowrie Castle," said the third, his big hand levelled at his brow to shade his eyes.

"Ay," said the first who had spoken, "there's the Castle, Venlaw, and at its doors we'll stand before we're an hour older. And I'll not say but it's worth coming these five thousand miles to do. For, bedad, there's no home like the old home."

"And there's no love like the old love," rejoined Venlaw, beneath his breath. But Benoni spoke nothing further but whistled gaily *Rob Roy's Return*.

An hour after there was loud knocking at the outer door of Cowrie Castle; and then, not waiting,—for the door was open— three visitors ascended the stone stairs. Benoni was leading. On the threshold of the door of the room where Jean sat, they paused, and the old man knocked, and then entered, followed by the others. Two women stood together by the loom. One started forward with a faint cry; the other hung back.

"I have brought them home, you see," said Benoni.

The foremost one held out her hand to him. "Yes, yes," she said, and her eyes shifted slowly from one to the other, as though she found it hard to be sure that they were there. Then she breathed hard. "But—but whaur's my brither?" she added —"my brither!"

Benoni spoke up gently. "I could not bring him. He could not come back to Scotland, if he would."

"Whaur's my brither?" she urged. Her

eyes fell upon Brian, but not yet in greeting. "You remember, Brian—Brian Kingley, that you helped him awa'; and the last time that I saw you was in this room, when you brocht my brither tae me. You went with him across the seas. Tell me, is he leevin'?"

Without a word Brian drew from his breast a letter, and handed it over to her, and his eyes were bent on her with strange longing. She took the letter, looked at the writing on it, and then thrust it into her bosom.

"There have been sorrow and troubles since you left here, Andrew Venlaw and Brian Kingley,—bitter troubles. You hae dune wrong to me ither and tae me. I hae waited until noo. . . . Tell me," she added, looking at neither, yet looking at them all, "were harsh things done atween ye, or atween my brither an' onyane o' ye?"

She was still solemn, and her eyes suddenly filled with tears, and the look upon her face was the suffering and endurance of years.

Andrew Venlaw spoke. "I wronged you, Jean Fordie. I believed you — believed you——"

She pieced out his sentence—"evil," she said. "Do you think I can ever forgie ye for that, Andrew Venlaw?"

He stood like one stunned, but strong. "I dare not ask it," he responded, "but I have come, like an honest man at least, to acknowledge my wrong."

Then Brian spoke. "You must forgive him, Jean Fordie—before God, you must! for he did no wilful wrong."

The woman behind Jean started forward. "It was me that leed tae him," she said, and stood still, trembling.

Jean waved her back gently.

Brian continued: "The beginning of the wrong was mine. I make no excuse for myself. I was wild and thoughtless and bad——"

"And bad," Jean repeated after him.

"I didn't know how much that—that kiss would cost you," he added; "and indeed I didn't know how much 'twould cost me." There was bitterness in his voice.

She smiled a strange smile. "What has it cost you?" she asked.

He threw his head back as though something had caught him at the throat, and then he smiled back at her strangely too. "Something that can't be reckoned by figures," he replied; "nor yet by years; but part of the account I keep by a scar on my shoulder and an awkward arm."

"A scar! from whom?" she interrupted; "from whom?"

"From your brother," he answered, after a moment's pause. "And had it been in the heart, and not the shoulder, I could have had no quarrel with it."

She started painfully. A sudden anxiety ruled her features. She looked at him for a moment searchingly. "Did ye fecht him," she said, "because o' me?"

"No, I did not fight," he answered. "There was not—time."

Her eyes dropped to the floor. "I was a young girl when you went away," she said at last to these silent men before her. "I'm a woman now, young eneuch to care what the world says about me, auld eneuch to endure a' it thinks. Elsie here has done a' she could tae undo her falsehood, and I hae forgiven her. . . . And noo," she added, and she held out one hand frankly yet sadly to Andrew, and another to Brian—"noo I'll forgie baith o' you."

She looked at Andrew seriously now; then dropped her gaze before the intense earnestness of his.

"Well," said Benoni here, with a grave lightness in his voice, "since we have done with sorrowful things, let us be joyful, as all home-comers should. And first, my dear, the showman claims your cheek, for he thinks he has earned one touch of it. He has tramped across the world, a meddlesome old man, with a flute under his arm, and his rarce show left behind him and growing rusty at Cowrie Castle."

Now, for the first time since they had entered the room, a light spread on Jean's face, and she leaned over and kissed Benoni on the cheek. "Is that all the pay you ask?" she said. "It is little."

"Ha! ha!" merrily laughed the old man in retort, "indeed, it's not all I'll ask, for it's long between now and Beltane fair again, and I've lived so much on heathen victuals, that I could eat each day six Scotch meals of your making; and those six Scotch meals I'll have, and more besides, with a bed under this roof and a little good liquor now and then as the thirst seizes me."

"Ye'll hae a' thrae," she answered; "as mony meals as it pleases ye—sic as they are—and no you alane, but Andrew Venlaw and Brian Kingley if they'll stay till I've laid the table, and made a hot cake in the ashes. For Elsie and I——" she looked round, and paused.

Elsie was gone. She had stolen away when the change in the talk occurred. She knew what misery she had caused, and while she also knew she had been forgiven, she could not face the look in the eye of the man whose love she longed for, and had sinned for, but who must always be far from her, till the end of her life and his. She went home to her idiot brother, and sat on the floor beside him, and said nothing. She was lonely with him, for he had his realm—his wild realm—of fancies; and she had only the stern world to fight; and her own past memories to face. The idiot fell asleep beside her, his great head lolling in her lap; and the hours went by, and still she sat there conjuring up that room she had left behind at the Castle, and those therein.

If they whom Elsie thought on were not merry, at least the insupportable constraint of the first few moments was gone, and they soon drifted into easy talk upon old days and old friends. They asked for her father, and here she gravely, and as Benoni thought, apprehensively, said that she expected him, but that he had gone far across the hills, and it was possible he might be late. They sat about the table eating, but they would drink no toasts, they said, until Black Fordie came.

At last they heard his rough footstep on the stair, and he entered boisterously on them. They all rose to their feet, as he glowered in astonishment at them, though he had known of Benoni's mission across the sea. The years had dealt hardly with him. His hair was very grey, his shoulders stooped, and his face wrinkled. Still the old sturdiness was there too, and his eyes flashed out sharp looks at the three men. Venlaw he had always liked. Brian he had never forgiven. Had he met him a year ago he would have killed him. Elsie cured that. Just now their presence acted on him strangely. His hand leaped out to Andrew's, and clutched it with a hungering eagerness, and then to Benoni, and it caught him by the shoulder. "You're verra welcome back, Andy," he said, "and I've a noggin waitin' for ye, Benoni, and no siccan a, ane as the lass has put on the table for ye. But it's in a bottle which naebody kens o' but mysel'."

He had not yet spoken to Brian, and still not looking at him, but with his eyes on Andrew, he said : " Ye hae cam frae the Arctic warld ; ye hae cam frae the land o' exiles. Did ye ken if they heard there o' a wastrel and villain, that carried the name o' Fordie ?"

"John Fordie," replied Andrew, firmly, "it's but few months since one of that name

laid hand in mine, and said : ' When yo set foot on the soil o' auld Scotland again, the first step ower the Border, get aff' yer horse, and gang doon on your knees, and kiss the ground for me, whether it be rock or heather ; for I'll never see the like o' that land. It's a land that God loves, and made for men, and no for vagabonds such as was I.' "

"Did he say that ?" interrupted the old man with a slight huskiness in his voice. "Did the hard-hearted scoondrel say that ?"

"That, John Fordie, and more. ' And when you got above Braithen town,' said he, ' stand still, and look down at it, and say : A man went out frae Braithen town like a thief in the dark, and he took a' his sins and his shame wi' him, and the bad luck that gang wi' baith ; but he left his heart ahint him,——' "

"Did the raff say that ?" cried the old man, interposing, and he struck his leg with his whip as though disturbed in mind ; for his was a stern nature, and it had been said of him, all his life, that he never forgave—and even yet he did not look at Brian.

"And this more, he said," continued Andrew,—" ' When you gang doon to the Shielside dip yer hand in the water, and whistle that song we used to sing as we paddled alang frae Cowrie Castle to Margaret's Brae, *For Ilka Man and Ilka Maid that Lives by Shielie Water ;* and when you see the Castle, and enter it, ye'll find a man they ca' Black Fordie. And he's a guid man, but he's a stern man ; and ye'll say to him that there's a lad at the Arctic Circle that, maybe, he'll never see again, wha wad gie ten years o' his life to say to his face, " Ye're a gran' man, John Fordie, and a bad day it was for you and for him, when he brocht shame on ye." And tak' his hand and gie him the grip o' the clan, and what mair be the will o' God.' "

The old man dropped into a chair, his hands on his knees, his head bent forward, his eyes upon the floor. " Did the lad say that ?" murmured he ; " did the laddie say that ?"

There was silence. Jean's face was turned pityingly away, and Brian had drawn slightly aside. Benoni seemed intent on his flute, which he was balancing in his fingers.

Presently the old man rose and walked over to Brian. "I'll no say that I loe the sicht o' yer face, Brian Kingley, for ye've done mair wrang than gnid tae me and mine ; but I'm willin' to let bygones be byganes, and there's my hand, an' ye'll take it !"

Brian clasped the extended hand. "You've got a son, John Fordie," said he, " whose name stands as high in that new land as it stood low in the old ; and you do well to let bygones be bygones, as others have nobly done before you." He glanced at Jean.

"And what's to be the end o' this ? O' your comin' back ?" the old man continued. "What hae ye come for ? Ye hae left the lad ahint ye. Which o' ye has came to tak' awa the lass, too. Ay, ye needna look, ye needna look, as if ye hadna sic a thocht in your heid ; but ye'll baith gang back to the land ye cam frae, wi'oot the lass—John Fordie's lass: for ye ken, Andy Venlaw, when ye should hae trusted ye disbelieved ; and siccan a fule as ye were ! ye ran awa. An' d' ye think ye'll mend that noo ? And for you, Brian Kingley, that comes o' gentle blood, ye did a thing——"

The girl stepped in between. "Faither," she said, "ye shall not. They hae come back —they hae come back, only to——"

"Ay, I ken weel what they hae cam back for ; the flame o' your cheeks is the meaning o' that ; but I'll no push the matter the nicht, whatever !"

Here Benoni tossed at them all a shrill note from his flute, and imitating Fordie's voice, said gaily: "When ye hae done prophesyin' and preachin', Black Fordie, and when you're ready to think aboot things for which you hae understanding, I'll tak' my noggin o' whusky oot o' yon unco bottle, that mane kens but yoursel'. For ye ken, that when it comes to marryin' and giein' in marriage o' the lass called Jean Fordie, ye're no the only man that has a voice i' the matter."

At this the other wheeled, and, with a startled and peculiar look, fixed his eyes on the showman. But Benoni had spoken lightly, and his face carried no special significance at the moment, and Fordie turned to his mission for the liquor.

But Jean had caught the unusual note in the proceeding, despite her own embarrassment at her father's words. After a moment, when they were all gathered about the table, ready to drink a toast of Fordie's making, she suddenly said, in a strange and meaning voice,—"Faither !"

Instantly both Benoni and Black Fordie turned to her. She had evidently accomplished what she desired. She changed her tone, and said, looking now only at John Fordie,—"What is your toast, faither ?"

And he, raising his glass, said : "To every frien' o' Scotland !"

"Wait," she urged. "And to every absent friend o' Scotland !"

"To every friend, and to every absent friend o' Scotland !" the old man repeated after a moment; and they drank in silence.

CHAPTER XIII.—"PEEBLES AT THE PLAY."

ALL Braithen soon knew of the return of the exiles, and because Venlaw and Brian came amicably together, and were amiably received at Cowrie Castle by Black Fordie as by his daughter, and Elsie had tried to undo what she had so illy done, the makers of scandal ceased its manufacture. But old women as they crooned in their doorways, the elders of the Kirk as they sauntered in the churchyard, and even the minister himself, discussed with serious eagerness the present passage of events. What Brian had done at Beltane Fair was not forgotten, nor was the quarrel that followed it. If Jean was innocent, it was clear she could not marry the man who had insulted her. If she was guilty she could not marry Andrew Venlaw ; and so jealously selfish is human nature, that very many of them had been glad if she had never married at all. And Jean herself ? Never once in all these eleven years had her heart faltered in its love of Brian. But yet there was a debt to Andrew ! He had distrusted her, but he had had some apparent cause, for she had not resented, that day of Beltane, Brian's shameful caress. The austere sincerity, the high honour, of this man impressed her deeply. He was worthy of her; he had always been worthy of her. And more : she knew that since a child he had been her lover, and had honourably followed upon her footsteps, and that through her, indirectly, the dreams of his life had been given up, and he had become the companion of savages. He had never been the ideal lover, but he had been persistent in a manly way; downright, gentle, and brave. Even now, as the days went on, she saw that he held himself in check. His manner to her was ever cheerful and kind, but he ventured on no sign of love. Yet, because she herself loved, she could read the signs in him, inconspicuous as he thought they were. She read Brian also with a pathetic kind of triumph. He had left her with a drunken trifler's kiss upon her lips, caring no more for her than for the silliest milk-maid in the hills. She knew now, beyond all doubt, that his heart was at her feet ; and she would have been an angel and not a woman if she had failed to appreciate the position. And the two men bore themselves towards each other with uncommon fairness. They had in them the soul of the game. The

"The Indian sends messages to her who loves Ironheart."

leevin' wi' savages, and keep the gristle i' your bones:" and he shook his head with a chuckle.

"I've had good days in the world, and many a land have I seen, and many a ship have I trod, and I've been a little of the gentleman, and very much of the vagabond, something of the fool, and a bit philosopher too, I hope. . . . And now I'm coming to the time when I must lay by with my old raree show and flute; and go out no more to wander."

"And to wanner nae mair," said Fordie, abstractedly.

"I did not think," the other continued, "that I should ever want back from your hands what's mine, but has been as yours for many a year, and——"

Rising suddenly to his feet, Fordie hoarsely interrupted him. "David," he said, "I kenned it was comin'. Seven-and-twenty years syne, you had sair trouble, and your bairn, new-born, was left mitherless. At that time my wife lost a bairn at its birth and she went mad for it, and we took yours—for you were far awa', a prisoner o' war—and we put it in her airms and she made it her ain, nursin' it at her ain breest. And it was lang afore ye cam back; and ye maun gang awa' again—for it was time o' war. And you said tae me, for the wife ne'er kenned it, that the child should be ours, for it had grown like our ain, and ye might never come back. And ye had mair dangers and hard fortunes; and when ye landed on England's soil again you had na a hawbee; and the bairn had got to loe us, and we to loe her."

Benoni raised his hand in protest, as though the remembrance of these things hurt him. There was a slight pause, and Fordie continued: "And ye became Benoni, the Italian showman, and when she's a woman

great North had made them too big for little jealousies now.

Brian ate his heart out in secret, for he saw that Jean was gentler to Andrew than to him; but when he met Andrew afterwards, he was always friendlier, in proportion to his private uneasiness.

Black Fordie and Benoni had their hours of suspense also. They also had their hours of moodiness—a thing uncommon to Benoni, at least. One day they sat alone in the Castle. Each knew that something was to be spoken, which had long lain hidden from the world.

"John Fordie," said the showman, at last, "there's a thing on which we have words to say to one another, after many years."

Fordie looked straight before him through the cloud of tobacco smoke, fiercely puffed forth, and said: "I know that weel, David."

"I'll not have many years to live, John."

"Ay, ay," interjected Fordie, dryly, "ye'll be growin' grey and stoopit. Ye'll no travel across the warld, and back again, and be the noo ye'd tell her a'—eh, David, and yo'd tak' her frae me, forbye."

"Fordie," brokenly said the other, "I did not think I should come to care so much, but I'd give the rest of my life to hear her call me *father* once."

"I have lost a son," mournfully responded the other, "and ye wad tak' frae me my dochter too."

"You've been a good father to her, Fordie, stern man though you are."

Fordie paced up and down the room twice or thrice, and then pausing before the other, said, as if speaking hurt him :- ·"If ye think it weel, David, I'll gie her tae ye ; I'll gie her tae ye—but think ye o' the lass hersel'."

Benoni rose, and laid a trembling hand on the other's arm. "I've been *David* for these few minutes, Fordie, and I have been weak —for I'm getting old—and I love the lass, God knows ! But I am wrong. She has had trouble enough. I'll not try her further.—— I've been a coward for a minute, Fordie, but, please Heaven,—no more !"

There was silence now. From the court-yard Jean's voice floated up through the open window of the room, and another voice with it. Both men caught their breaths in their throats.

"She shall never know through me, Fordie, while you live, though I told her she should be told my story some day ; but she'll be leaving us both, maybe, and 'tis better as it is, I doubt not." And Benoni smiled sadly out towards the voices floating up to them. The two men shook hands silently.

But they were both wrong concerning Jean. She suspected the truth. And in future days, when Black Fordie was in his last illness, all was told, and in losing one father she found another.

But now a thing more important to her happiness was near. It perplexed Fordie and Benoni ; it made havoc with the peace of Venlaw and Brian ; it compelled into action all Jean's womanliness and character.

Down in the courtyard Andrew Ven-law walked with Jean. The weeks and months had passed, and to-morrow again was Beltane Fair. The time of Andrew's leave was up. He must return to his duties in that far-off region of Hudson's Bay or make up his mind to remain where he was ; and to remain where he was meant to marry Jean ; and to marry Jean meant that Brian must go. These things they had not said to each other,

yet they were in the minds of all. In the town of late Andrew's name had been coupled much with Jean's, and this they both knew, and Black Fordie and Benoni knew it, and both of these had spoken in Jean's presence concerning her and Andrew, as though they were accepted of each other. At last, by a hundred little things, Andrew came to be-lieve that Jean would not say No to him if he asked her. It did not make him proud ; it humbled him, because he read the true mean-ing of her gentle acquiescence. Her affection, her respect, her sense of justice were with him, but her love was with his comrade.

"And now," he said to her, his mind at last made up after some heavy hours, "I'm goin' back, Jean, the day after Beltane Fair."

"Back whaur, Andrew ?" she said, a white-ness spreading on her face.

"Back to the land they call 'God's Coun-try,'" said he—"to the Arctic circle, or thereabouts."

She drew slightly from him, but she did not speak.

"Have you nothing to say to my going ?" he added, with a painful smile.

"I—I am very sorry ; but must you go ?"

"There's only one thing that would keep me," he replied.

"Li ted her hand to his lips."

"And what's that, Andrew?" she asked.

"The love of a woman," was his reply; "of a good woman."

"Do you mean, Andrew, that if that—guid woman would marry you, you would stay?" A greyness came about her temples. It was harder than she thought.

"Ay, ay, lass," he said, dropping back into the old dialect of his youth: "if she would marry me."

She came slowly to him, and laid her hand upon his arm. "Andrew," she said, "Andrew,—the woman—will—marry you."

His breast heaved, his arms twitched at his side, his massive body drew up, and he looked down at her with a great yearning.

"Ay, ay, lassie," he responded, the roughness of feeling in his tone, "I ken she would marry me. That is one thing, and it has made me think o' heaven; but would she love me, does she love me, and me alone? That is anither thing."

His eyes searched hers, and she dropped them before him.

"She wad try to loe ye, Andrew," she rejoined.

"There is another man," he said with a sigh, "and he has a good heart. He is generous and brave, and the woman loves him."

"Oh, hush!" she said, and she raised her fingers towards his lips, a scared look in her face. "Ye maunna speak o't," she added.

They stood silent, a little away from each other, for a moment.

"Will you walk with me?" he asked.

Without a word she turned, and passed with him into the shadow of the yews. They did not speak. Presently, Andrew, looking out upon the road, saw a figure coming. He wheeled upon her gently, and said: "The day after Beltane I shall go."

She did not instantly reply, but stretched out her hand and raised her eyes to his, with a look of solemn thankfulness which he loved to remember years after. But he knew the immeasurable distance between friendship and love.

"Wait here," he said; "wait just here for a little while, will you?"

"Yes," she replied, "as lang as ye will; but why?"

He did not reply in words, but looked out upon the road, down which Brian was coming. She understood. Strong, deep-natured as she was, she shivered slightly with timidity.

"Oh, no, no, not now, Andrew," she urged.

But he, without a word, and with a grave courtesy, lifted her hand to his lips, and, with head uncovered, drew away from her. He walked steadily on till he met Brian. He paused for a moment, stretched out his hand, and said: "She is waiting for you, Brian, in the yews below."

"Waiting—for me—Venlaw?" said Brian, growing pale.

"I'm going away to the Company's land two days after Beltane, but you'll be staying here."

"I'll—be staying—here," Brian repeated, as the matter dawned upon him. He could say no more; but the two men caught hands, and parted suddenly, both to begin life again.

An hour after, Andrew stood by the old Dominie's grave looking down at it with a gentle sadness, gentle and sad as only a strong man can be. He had squared all accounts. The Dominie's wishes had been fulfilled. The money left him he had handed over to Katie Dryhope and her sister Maggie; he had refused his own happiness from a high sense of justice. There was nothing more to do but to go away. He thought that as he stood by the grave.

And Brian Kingley walked with Jean, his arm about her, in the shadows of the yews.

The next morning was Beltane Fair. Braithen was dancing upon the green. There were fiddlers many, but you could hear above the jaunty scraping of the catgut the soft joyful note of a flute. It seemed to have caught an exhilarating something from the warm breeze, which, sweeping across the braes and down the wimpling Shiel, ran round the valley where Braithen lay, blithe with the sunshine. Now and then it caught the gay ribands of some laughing lass, or lifted, always modestly, the simple folds of a pretty skirt. And the loose flowing hair of man and woman, it blew in warm enjoyment along the undulations of the dance. About old Benoni's raree show boys sat munching gingerbread. Horsemen moved in and out, and on the stroke of noon a troop of His Majesty's cavalry swung slowly through the streets, bringing with them some gay prisoners of war, who were being transferred from a post further south to Braithen. It seemed almost the same crowd that we saw twelve years before. It might, indeed, have seemed the same day, save that Benoni's hair was greyer and his cheek more wrinkled, though his eye was just as gay. And it did not grow duller because he heard the gossiping of some dames behind him discussing the fortunes of one very dear to him. The twinkle in it, indeed, had something a little ironical. But the groups went dancing on before him, and everyone said that Benoni had never played so well. From the way he looked to right and left from time to time, it was clear he was expecting somebody; and one had known when his expectations were fulfilled by the very immediate impulse he gave to his music.

Presently among the gossiping and staring crowd there passed Jean and Brian, followed by John Fordie and Andrew Venlaw. They came into the circle of dancers. Brian led Jean out gravely into the centre, and danced a measure with her lightly yet sedately. And when it was finished, with all eyes upon them, all dancing stopped around them, he kissed her full upon the mouth: and that was how Braithen knew that Brian Kingley and Jean Fordie were to marry.

CHAPTER XIV.—THE RETURN.

It was so still the Fort seemed sleeping. The intemperate sunshine fell upon it ardently; its walls, its roofs, the very mortar creasing its stones, were soaked in heat and silence. A slumberous dog caught at an intrusive gnat, the great blue-bottles of a short-lived summer boomed on the panes, the chain of a bear rattled lazily, as Bruin turned to a new position of idleness in his yard. Human life seemed absent. The windows and the doors of the Fort were open; no sound came from them save from one room, and then it was only the ticking of a clock.

Yet, if one had looked into the cool dusk of that window there would have been seen a strange thing. A girl half-sat, half-knelt, upon the floor, her eyes upon the clock. She was motionless, she was silent, save that had you also knelt beside her you would have heard her heart beating up against her bosom like a muffled pendulum. She was watching, waiting; and though lips have sometimes a trick of silence, hearts have the impertinent habit of crying out. This girl's heart was calling, so loudly, indeed, that a traveller approaching the Fort from a distant point in the horizon must easily have heard it, if the voice of a heart is like that of the lips. Perhaps he did hear it, but not in the fashion which would go for evidence in a court of law. We cannot swear to soundless voices; yet sometimes they speak so plainly; that one in telling what they said might de clare to speaking the truth, Heaven helping him.

The traveller paused when his eyes fell upon Waiting Mountain. It was his first welcome home.—— This was his home now, and should be, to that hour when the father of his biographer should bid him a staunch God-speed upon the great journey man takes when he goeth to his long home. The mountain slept; but he could see its breath rising in hot palpitations, and come floating towards him, a fragrant wafture on his cheek. As the smell of some perfumed letter, or the balm of some forgotten relic, floats up to a man's nostrils as he fumbles among old tokens, and his past heaves on him like a ghost, so Andrew Venlaw stands still in the flowered plain, and faces suddenly the wilderness of his past, which, by the spirit of an unconquerable manhood, he had made into a garden: for he had learned and performed according to the great charm, the noble spirit of peace, which is self-sacrifice. He had come back to return no more; but here lay a vast field of endeavour, and on yonder fort there flew the flag of the bold adventurers of the North, the splendid free-booters of the wilds: his heart swelled big. He was a chief of hardy comrades, a leader of men.

He had left his companions behind, and had hurried on that he might reach the Fort alone, not that he might brood upon matters of retrospect or affection, but to face the hard duties of his future, the possible solitariness of the rest of his natural life, with that iron heart credited to him by his people and the heathen.

He came on. Beyond the belt of woods to his right were the Indian lodges. His mind hung over them for a moment. He framed some new conditions of policy then and there; but first and last, and interwoven with these thoughts, was a wholesome, generous solicitude regarding Summer-Hair, her father, and their people. His thoughts dwelt upon Red Fire for a moment. Red Fire should be his friend. Red Fire should marry Summer-Hair. No doubt he had done so. Here Venlaw paused. Well, so much the better for Red Fire and for Summer-Hair and for—he paused again, and presently pushed on, as though some thought had disturbed him, angered him, and he was walking over it.

In the south, where he had been detained in consultation with some of his superior officers, he sent word by couriers carrying the yearly mails that he would arrive at Fort Saviour about this time, and again the previous night he had urged a courier on, and whoever has followed his fortunes closely must know without telling that the girl within that room at the Fort, watching the day go round the clock, was Summer-Hair.

When she knew that Venlaw was coming back, and, further, knew the time, they had noticed the wine colour of her face grow fainter. The spirit of suspense had entered into her eyes, and devoured her cheek.

The afternoon wore on. There was a stir about the fort. She heard excited voices. She sprang to the window and looked out. HE was coming, and her heart cried out with a great joy, for he came—alone.

And she turned and sped through the yard of the Fort and out across the plains, away from it and him, to the lodges of her people.

But when Venlaw came to the lodge where she was, to tell her how he sorrowed for her father's death (which had occurred while he was away), he was amazed to see in what dignity and reserve she carried herself. Perhaps, he said to himself, loneliness and bereavement had accomplished this. And then, maybe, Red Fire's marriage with a less notable girl than herself had helped to make her graver too.

But had Venlaw been a vainer man happiness had come to him sooner; and so likewise to Summer-Hair. It is possible, however, that neither would have deserved the other so much if, before a certain day of a year later, Venlaw had said to her the few simple words which go for the making or breaking of lives. How far he was moved by love, and how far by gratitude, is not to be told here; and he was ever too much the man to make the measurement for himself. Still, it was said of him throughout his life that he had a wonderful memory. That so, and being what he was, when he looked back—but no——!

THE END.

www.ingramcontent.com/pod-product-compliance
Lightning Source LLC
Chambersburg PA
CBHW022022080426
42733CB00007B/681

* 9 7 8 3 7 4 1 1 9 3 7 3 6 *